The Secure Solution

Creating a High-Quality Retirement in a Low-Interest-Rate World

Telton W Hall, CFP®

IGNITE PRESS
Fresno, CA

Published in the United States by
Ignite Press
5070 N 6th St. #189
Fresno, CA 93710
www.IgnitePress.us

ISBN: 978-1-953655-49-3 (Amazon Print)
ISBN: 978-1-953655-50-9 (IngramSpark) PAPERBACK
ISBN: 978-1-953655-51-6 (IngramSpark) HARDCOVER
ISBN: 978-1-953655-52-3 (E-book)

For bulk purchase and for booking, contact:

Advanced Financial Planning

415 North Main Ste #206
Cedar City, Utah 84720
afplanning.com
marty@afplanning.com
435-263-0550

Library of Congress Control Number: 2020925854

Cover design by Salman Sarwar
Edited by Reid Maruyama
Interior design by Jetlaunch

This book is dedicated to:

My parents who got me started and
my wife who has seen me through.

My Parents, Darwin and Shirlene. Around age 9, my mom taught me about mutual funds. Then my dad shared with me a couple lines from his favorite book, Little Britches by Ralph Moody: "God planned this earth so that it would yield every single thing that the people on it need. But He was careful to plan it so that it would only yield its wealth in exchange for labor… Some work almost entirely with their hands; some labor almost entirely with their brains; though most of us have to use both." The strategies and information in this book continue to be my brain-labor of love.

My wife, April. Based on all available evidence, April appears to be completely incapable of entertaining the slightest doubts in my ability to persevere and succeed.

Table of Contents

Foreword: Dr. Craig Israelsen vii

Chapter 1: Spoiler Alert and the Fish Pond 1

Chapter 2: Did You Just Say "Negative Rates"? 7

Chapter 3: Mortgages, Math, and Emotions 17

Chapter 4: The Thirty-Trillion-Ton Elephant 23

Chapter 5: Say Hello to LIBOR and Prime 27

Chapter 6: Mortgages, Treasuries, and the Fed 31

Chapter 7: Inflation 43

Chapter 8: Auto Loans 47

Chapter 9: CDs and Savings Rates 51

Chapter 10: Short-Term Bonds 59

Chapter 11: Short-Term (Three- or Five-Year) Fixed Annuities . . . 65

Chapter 12: Lifetime Payment Annuities 71

Chapter 13: Indexed Annuities 77

Chapter 14: Variable Annuities 85

Chapter 15: Tool Belts, Tactical Allocations, and Bond Credit Ratings 93

Chapter 16: Index Allocations 103

Chapter 17: The Agg (Bloomberg-Barclays Aggregate Bond Index) . . . 111

Chapter 18: TIPS (Treasury Inflation-Protected Securities Index) . . . 117

Chapter 19: International Bonds Index . . . 121

Chapter 20: Natural Resources and Commodities Indexes . . . 127

Chapter 21: Exchange-Traded Real Estate . . . 133

Chapter 22: U.S. Stock Indexes: Large, Mid, and Small Capitalization . . . 141

Chapter 23: U.S. Stock in a Low-Interest-Rate Environment . . . 145

Chapter 24: Non-U.S. Stock Indexes . . . 149

Chapter 25: Transforming Indexes into Strategic Allocations . . . 153

Chapter 26: Why Mitigating Market Volatility and Maintaining Growth Potential Matters . . . 157

Chapter 27: The 7Twelve Portfolio . . . 163

Chapter 28: Factor Investing . . . 169

Conclusion: Take Heart and Take Aways . . . 177

Quick Reference Glossary . . . 185

About the Author . . . 201

Foreword

Having known Telton Hall for a decade, I know his heart and trust his insights.

The modern global economic system can be somewhat baffling. Telton provides an insightful overview of *how things work*. With that Econ 101 refresher under your belt, the logical steps in building a system for secure retirement income make more sense. You'll have a better understanding of the *why* behind the *what* and *how* of investing and retirement income as we move forward in a world where low interest rates may be the norm for some time.

With a bolstered knowledge of how financial things *work*, you will naturally understand that financial things may temporarily *not work*. It is during those times that your prudent game plan for building a secure retirement income will be tested by fears and emotions. Telton's approach to this book anticipates those moments—but in an optimistic way.

When we understand how financial systems and investment products work over the long haul, we are less likely to bail out of our plan simply because of a short-term hiccup or a scary headline. This is REALLY important because the greatest risk to most investment portfolios (sadly) is knee-jerk bad behavior of the investor—not the investment markets that the portfolio is actually invested in. For this reason, increasing our understanding of the mechanisms of investing is so valuable. We naturally become better investors as our understanding increases.

Additionally, Telton Hall is a master storyteller. That talent makes this highly educational book rather delightful reading. He translates his life experiences into life lessons and shows how they meaningfully apply to our financial lives. More importantly, his life lessons reveal the real Telton—a man without guile whose daily walk is to assist and help his fellow travelers.

You're fortunate to have Telton's book in your hands.

Dr. Craig Israelsen,
Barron's Magazine and *Financial Planning Magazine* Author
7Twelve Portfolio Developer
Woodbury School of Business Executive-in-Residence

Chapter 1

Spoiler Alert and the Fish Pond

"Spoiler Aleeeert!"

That is what my nine-year-old son yells each time I start to describe a movie so the family can vote on what to watch. So just a heads up, spoiler alert, I want to share the plot of this book with you right up front. No fanfare. Here it is.

The Secure Solution is: Knowledge and Strategies.

- *Knowledge* to help you avoid costly mistakes, by understanding:
    - The Fed
    - Interest rates
    - Investments
    - Market indexes
    - Retirement products
- *Strategies* to give you the profit potential and risk mitigation you will need on your savings and investments

I am convinced that this combination of education and implementation is essential to creating a high-quality retirement for yourself.

The Secure Solution is *not* about speculative investments. You are likely bombarded by partial-truths on Cryptocurrency (like Bitcoin etc.), "hot penny-stock" opportunities, "The Day-Trading Secrets of Billionaire's," and "One Thousand Reasons Why You

Should Sell Everything and Buy Gold." That is all interesting and is based on some fragments of reality. Those investments are enticing, exciting...and highly speculative. They really could be great, or they could be an irreparable mistake. I think the solutions to a secure retirement are less thrilling in the short-term; instead, I believe the right solutions will have long histories. They will be research-based, systematically applied, and absolutely wonderful over the long term.

My son is not here to stop me, so I'm going to go ahead and "spoil" some more: The next two stories I'm going to tell you have happy endings (one I'll tell here, and another in Chapter 2). They were terrifying for me at the time, but don't worry. They both took place on balconies during the Great Recession of 2008–2009. The lessons, and all the tiny details of the events, are a vivid part of my life and my decision making.

The Fish Pond

My daughter's face looked pale. Her eyes were closed. She was almost smiling, her features relaxed. Her face was 10 inches underwater. I have seen corpses' faces less pale than my daughter's face was in those moments before I ripped her little body up and out of the fish pond.

Three scarlet autumn leaves floated in the small "fish pond" that my friend had just finished creating in a section of his backyard. The leaves were large and beautiful. In a calmer moment, the leaves had hovered on the surface of the water like hawks over a mountain slope. Beautiful. Elegant. A reminder of the beauty in every season; the grace in every creation. The leaves had flown from the scene of the accident now. They cowered on top of each other on the near-side of the pond while I sprinted across pink flagstone to the far-side. To the pale skin. To the little body. To the peaceful face.

As I pause right there in the story, you can see why I gave you the spoiler alert. I'm going to back up a few months before the "fish pond" incident to Spring of 2009. I was in conversation with my sister-in-law. My daughter and her daughter were both about a year old. She was trying to convince me to let her teach our babies "how to swim."

"You can't teach a baby to swim," I told my sister-in-law. "Even if you did see it on YouTube," I added with a laugh. It was the beginning of summer and my sister-in-law, a swim teacher, was considering teaching *her* baby and *my* baby to "swim."

She looked at me from under her furrowed brow, "I can too."

"I'm not buying it," I said. Truthfully, I was really intrigued, but we all know it's improper brother-in-law etiquette to immediately tell your sister-in-law when she's being brilliant. I was having some fun, so I said, "They can't talk, they can't walk, and they obviously have no knowledge base to start learning to swim."

She knew I was interested. She also knew that I had so easily forgotten the months that she and my wife had been pregnant, "Actually, your baby was 'swimming' for nine months before you ever saw her. She's already learned how. Once you learn, you don't forget. She can't walk and she can't run, but I'll show her that swimming is 'just like riding a bike.'"

Well, how do you disagree with that persuasive wit and logic? One or two times a week during the summer, my sister-in-law would work with my daughter and her daughter in the pool and incrementally my daughter "regained" her comfort with the water. When she was placed in the water, she would hold her breath, with her eyes closed, and then allow the buoyancy of her lungs to turn her from face-down to face-up. Then she would patiently wait as her buoyancy would lift her to the surface. When her face broke the surface she would take a breath, laugh, and be ready to do it again.

Now back to the evening of the fish pond incident.

Bordered by beautifully arranged flagstone, the fish pond was a new addition in the far back corner of the yard. All the adults were up on the balcony having dinner. My daughter had escaped the balcony. My wife and I looked around for her. My left palm grasped the rough-finished redwood deck railing as I saw my baby in the fish pond. *Jump this railing!* was my first thought. I was raised on a small ranch in Utah. Our little town took pride in knowing every arroyo, nook, and canyon of the three mesas that surrounded our mountain valley. We took pride in hard work and honesty. For my siblings and I, we also took pride in jumping fences. Climbing fences is good, but it's slow. If a steer is upset with you, then getting immediately on the other side of the fence became pretty natural for us. Our rule was, "If I can get a hand on the top rail, then I can clear the fence."

Clearing the balcony railing would be easy but the balcony was built upon a pile of rhino-size boulders that gave me no place to land. *Won't work* metered across my brain. I turned, and ran across the balcony. The dinner party froze. I raced. I headed for the stairs down, but did not touch them. From the top step I landed on the grass and left a green and brown streak on the knee of my khakis as I pivoted to head back towards the fish pond. Toward the calm pale face of what I thought was my drowning daughter.

The leaves had been floating peacefully, gracefully, on the water's surface. Now they were bunched up, cowering, on the nearside of the pond. The splash of water from my daughter's entry into the pond had turned the pinkish hues of the flagstone dark and red.

I could not reach my daughter yet, as she was on the far-side of the pond. Instead, I watched from my blurred and terrified vantage point as my daughter's pale peaceful face turned toward the light, then started to move upward. Her relaxed body lifted toward the surface. Doing what she had prepared beforehand to do. As her face broke the surface, my hands reached her body. Her eyes just started to open, and I pulled her up, out, and to my chest. I was soaked in gratitude as I held her sopping body to me tightly. When I pulled her away to look at her face, she was not laughing or giggling, but she was also not scared. She was uncomfortable, surprised, shaken-up, even bothered. Yet, I was terrified. Thanks to her preparation, she was not scared.

And that, my friends, is what this book is about: preparing you to achieve retirement success in a low-interest and potentially high-inflation-rate environment. Your retirement will not be in the financial environment that we have been accustomed to for the last 30 years. It's going to be in the environment of the present and the next 30 years. So you might need to rethink and relearn some things. This book is truly meant to be digestible education. Milk with a little bit of meat. Yes, I will get into the details on the global economic system, interest rates, indexes and financial products, but I will try to keep it as simple as possible. To reference my daughter's experience, she and her cousin did not need to master all the swim strokes, they only needed a certain level of knowledge and preparation in order to be safe and have fun. That's what we are going for here—education that can provide you with a secure solution for your retirement.

Did you know the plural of index has two versions?
Latin form: indices. English form: indexes.
Look how much you're learning already!

I'm also going to throw in some stories. I can't help it. I love stories, I love people's experiences, I love literature (I actually had a very hard time choosing between financial planning and being an English teacher), and I love helping people get the information they need to make smart decisions. Thanks for joining me.

Now let's talk about interest rates.

Chapter 2

Did You Just Say "Negative Rates"?

"What the heck is that?" is the usual question I get asked when my friends and clients hear a Fed Committee member, a news media outlet, or the U.S. president talking about "negative interest rates." Over the last several years, especially during mid-2020, there has been a fair amount of publicity, concern, and questions around interest rates and in particular negative interest rates. Understandably so, as it's a whole new financial world we're living in. Negative interest is a good place for starting to understand the rates, policies, drivers, and economic environment we will all have to navigate. I'll outline five basic concepts to get us started.

Concept One:

In a completely free economy, nobody sets a negative interest rate—a structure where I pay you to keep my money. Negative interest rates and zero interest rates only exist in an economic world ruled by Central or Federal Banks. However, in a federal bank economy, the Federal Open Market Committee (referred to as: the FOMC or "the Fed") sets or adjusts rates, to create a certain effect in the economy. There are actually a few ways that they could create "negative" interest rates. We'll cover one of those in this chapter.

Beginning with the Federal Reserve Act of 1913, the Federal Reserve Bank System has the authority and the responsibility to establish and change monetary policy to promote national economic health, price stability, and growth. The phrase, "Monetary Policy", refers to three different levers that the Fed can adjust:

- Open Market Operations
- The Discount Rate
- Reserve Requirements

I will focus on Open Market Operations. When I reference the "Fed Funds rate" (also called the "Fed Funds Target" rate or the "Fed Rate") it is a rate that is *set* and *adjusted* by the Federal Open Market Committee. The FOMC decides what actions to take and then directs the Federal Reserve Banks to implement and enforce those actions. Because it dictates the actions of the Federal Reserve Banks, the FOMC is often just called "the Fed". The FOMC sets the Fed Funds rate based on the tactics it has decided to employ.

The FOMC is made up of the following voting members:

- It is a board of 12 seats
    - Seven seats are the members of the Federal Reserve Board of Governors (Some of the actions taken by the Fed, like bank Reserve Requirements, are only voted on by this 7 member Board of Governors, some are voted on by all 12 members—for simplicity, and because the 7 Board of Governors members are the majority of the 12 FOMC members, I will simply refer to the FOMC throughout this book)
    - One seat is for the president of the Federal Reserve Bank of New York
    - Four remaining seats rotate, one from each group, between the presidents of the Federal Reserve Banks in:

- Boston, Philadelphia, and Richmond
- Cleveland and Chicago
- Atlanta, St. Louis, and Dallas
- Minneapolis, Kansas City, and San Francisco

- This board meets at least eight times a year to review economic data and to set the Fed Funds rate (also known as a target rate)

The far-reaching financial impact of the Federal Reserve Banks, the FOMC, and their monetary policy are what make negative interest rates even a possibility and zero or near-zero interest rates a reality.

The far-reaching financial impact of the Federal Reserve Banks, the FOMC, and their monetary policy are what make negative interest rates even a possibility and zero or near-zero interest rates a reality.

Concept Two:

The economic philosophy around this type of management of the economy is pretty straight forward. The Federal Funds rate is a "monetary policy" tool that begins with banks and trickles down to consumers. Theoretically, when there is an excess of growth and price inflation, the FOMC can raise interest rates to slow things down. Conversely, they can lower interest rates in order to stimulate economic growth. Lowering the interest rate has been far and away the most consisted go-to play in recent years. Actually, it's been the go-to move for the last 30+ years! Lowering interest rates reduces financing and borrowing costs, and this is supposed to encourage more investing, mortgaging, building, and spending. Most importantly, the Great Recession of 2008–2009 set the new precedent that during any economic scare the FOMC will plunge rates to 0%-.25% and will keep them there for an extended period of time.

Below is a chart of the Fed Funds rate over the last 65 years. One of the keys to retirement success and retirement income longevity is understanding why the FOMC does what it does. Most importantly, over the course of this book, I'll try to help you address how the Fed Funds rate may affect you. For now, just take note of the ultra-low rates after the '08–'09 recession. It stayed at zero or near zero for eight years. Then, notice the small increases that started in 2016 until March of 2020, *KABOOM*, all the way back down to zero as soon as the uncertainty of the pandemic hit. As of the writing of this book the Fed Funds rate is still zero or near zero. This is right in line with the new Federal Reserve playbook, and keeping rates low for a long time, with only nominal increases, is their new favorite play.

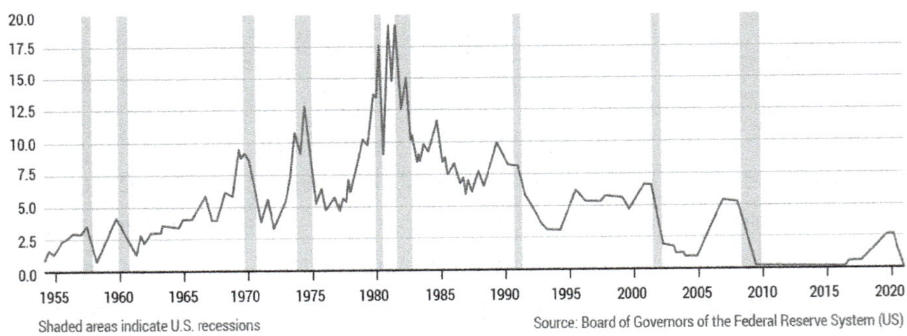

So it can't go any lower than zero, right?

Concept Three:

One theory of negative interest rates is that the Fed could set the Fed Funds rate at less than 0%. This, in effect, means that large banks would get paid by the Federal Reserve when loaning out more than their reserves. In a normal interest rate environment that would be a no-no. If a bank loans out more than its reserves it has to borrow money from other banks or the Federal Reserve Bank, at the Fed Funds rate, to replenish its reserves. If the Fed Funds rate is negative, banks would be incentivized to loan out more than their reserves. The theory is that banks would take actions to get rid of extra deposits. They could do that by making lots of loans at low interest rates. They could also lower deposits by de-incentivizing you to save with them. Perhaps even charging you interest to hold your money for you. This philosophy uses the theory that low interest rates stimulate the economy but then goes a big step further. It basically says, "If lowering interest rates helps people make more purchases and invest, imagine how the economy will boom if we charge people to save! Everyone will be spending and borrowing like crazy and the economy will take-off." That is a simplified way to explain the core of the concept.

Concept Four:

Thankfully, the U.S. does not have to be the first to try this experiment. In 2014, the European Central Banks attempted to mitigate their debt crisis with negative interest rates. They were followed by Sweden, Denmark, Switzerland, and in 2016, Japan's central bank decided to use this as well. So far, these experiments suggest that negative interest rates did not create tremendous benefits, and there are substantial negative effects, particularly on retirement systems. Just think about a pension fund that builds their payment promises around historical interest rates averaging 5% to 6%, then take them through 5, 10, or 15 years of very low rates. That pension is going to struggle. This has a negative impact on retirees. Negative rates also create a distortion of the lending system, and of course, negative rates are a detriment to savers overall.

Concept Five:

Consumer sentiment. While lowering interest rates seems to lead people to respond with an attitude of optimism for new opportunities, negative interest rates seem to create the opposite emotional reaction, causing folks to really pull back on their enthusiasm. As consumers we tend to lose confidence in a system that charges us to save.

So far, the Fed has demonstrated they are aware of these negative impacts, and are not inclined to use negative interest rates as a solution. However, the fact that this is even a conversation gives us a strong indication where interest rates will be, and obviously they won't be high. Hopefully they are not negative. So that leaves you with near-zero rates with potentially small increases in rates over-time.

I can't emphasize enough how impactful this is to you and your goals. The interest rate environment in which you will retire, is virtually the exact opposite of the interest rate environment retirees have had over the last 30 years. It is imperative that you create or update your retirement plan to address this.

The reality that we are talking about negative interest rates should be a reminder that the U.S. economy is not perfect. We'll talk about those imperfections. First, let me take a soapbox moment right here: I personally believe in the U.S. economy. Throughout this book I will address some of the major hurdles that we face. However, I do not see any retirement planning benefits of a doomsday approach. When I walk you through the challenges we're up against, please do not think I am talking about the collapse of the _______. You can fill in the blank with whatever the scare-tactic marketing of the day is: the dollar, the economy, real estate, government, the stock market—whatever you've heard is going to collapse. When it comes to retirement planning, by definition we are planning that you, me, the economy, the government, and the pursuit of happiness, will all still be here in five, ten, twenty, and thirty years. I think the economy will still be here. In order to accomplish your goals, you will need to be part of it. Betting on its demise is not going to get you through a long happy retirement. Please, keep that perspective in mind when I am talking honestly about the challenges we'll have to navigate together.

The U.S. economy will continue long-term to be strong, resilient, and robust, but we are all keenly aware of its imperfection. That leads me to story time.

THE TITANIC

As promised, I have another story that happened on a balcony. My experiences as a young financial advisor walking side by side with my clients through 2008 and 2009 became the core driver behind the strategies in this book.

I started my career at the brink of the last recession. We had a couple good years and I gained some of my first precious clients, families that I love and still work with today. Then we plunged into what is known as the Great Recession, the massive "Financial Meltdown," and things got scary. I was terrified and tense. Accounts were losing money. Things were not working like they were supposed to. Client's retirements were at risk. I cared about these people! Financial advisors were leaving the business in hoards—a bunch of the seasoned advisors and most, if not all the younger advisors were throwing in the towel. How could you help people when it felt like the rules had just changed, nobody knew the new rules, and nothing was working. Three advisors that I knew personally told me, "Telton, I can't live like this; this job is going to kill me." At that time, I had no words of encouragement. I could only close my eyes and silently nod in agreement.

Dave and Lucille were some of my first clients. Like most, they had both worked hard their entire lives. Dave was highly successful in his field, loved his job, and honestly hadn't put much thought into retiring or what planning for retirement might look like. Then Lucille was diagnosed with a debilitating disease, and as it progressed, she began to lose more and more mobility. She was unable to continue working in *her* beloved and successful profession. When they came to me, Dave's deepest desire was to retire from *his* profession to spend his retirement travelling with Lucille—nothing extravagant, just visiting family in the North East, taking a cruise, making sure to spend quality time with friends and loved ones before it was too late.

Dave's second goal, even though statistically very unlikely due to her health, was to make sure Lucille would be taken care of if he passed before she did. He was worried that in a time when the economy was showing signs of slowing down, their money set aside for retirement wouldn't last their lifetime, let alone allow for the additional expense of travel.

So, I worked with them to put together a prudent plan, Dave retired, and then the economy and the markets plummeted. Accounts we thought were good, were not. We lost money, everybody lost money. Strategies that were good, felt tenuous. I remember going over to Dave and Lucille's house to talk to them. I drove slowly up the hill to their house. What do you say about the future when you're trapped in the trauma of the present and the recent past?

We visited on the balcony looking out over a yard that Dave beautifully maintained. I told Dave that I was worried whether I had done the right things to keep their retirement funds secure. We talked openly about the issues. I gripped the balcony railing for support as I discussed the economic crash, the market collapse, investment losses, and what felt like insurmountable fear. It felt like the world we knew was sinking around us. The railing on their balcony was smooth, white, and elegant. My distraught mind thought, *This must feel like the Titanic.*

Dave had put on a *Man from Snowy River*-style hat when we walked out onto the balcony. He had been looking down as I spoke, but when he responded, he tipped his head up enough to look at me. Kind eyes, under bushy grey eyebrows. He said, "More's coming in than going out each month. Because of your help I don't think that's going to change. Telton, that's all we need."

I found strength in that steadfast simplicity and sincerity.

That time period was beyond distressing; however, using, improving, and perfecting the battle-tested concepts I'll share in this book we had created a successful retirement. We had set up a retirement plan that allowed Lucille and Dave to not only travel, but also maintain the lifestyle they wanted in retirement without the stress and fear of outliving their money. Then, in a strange twist of fate, Dave's premonition came true. He passed away unexpectedly only a few years into retirement. As of the writing of this book, Lucille is still alive and living comfortably near her grown children and grateful for the extra retirement time she and Dave spent together. During our review meetings, she always greets me with, "There's my money man. I've been spending a lot. Do I have any left?"

I get to smile and answer, "Yes."

My experience with Dave and Lucille was real life. It was personal. It created the lens I look through for all of my clients. Lessons from that time-period illuminate the approaches described in this book. I hope it shines some light on your retirement success.

Chapter 3

Mortgages, Math, and Emotions

Now that we've started to understand low and even negative Fed Funds rates in the context of how the Great Recession reshaped me, you, the economy, interest rates and the FOMC's strategies, let us address something else that was talked about A LOT in the last recession: mortgages. Especially in a low-interest-rate environment, having, or not having, a mortgage could be an integral part of optimizing your retirement income strategy. One of the biggest questions I field consistently and repeatedly is, "Should I take funds from my retirement account, at retirement, to pay off my mortgage?"

It's a valid question that shows the person is engaged in making smart decisions about their retirement. The answer has far reaching ramifications. I'm going to walk you through the math but I would also have you think about, and start to clarify, your own core values around money.

Especially during volatile economic and stock market conditions, there emerges a strong emotional drive for security. This emotional driver makes paying off one's mortgage feel like the priority. One of my goals for this chapter is to help you recognize the strong emotional reasons that factor into your retirement goals, your decision making, and your psychology around your decisions. Perhaps most importantly, let's start to understand that it's not a bad thing to have these emotional reasons if you become aware of them and purposefully let them enlighten your decisions.

Like many things financial, the decision factors are 80% or 90% emotional and the remaining 10% or 20% mathematical.

Much like a coach will call time out and draw up a play to provide clarity during a barn-burner basketball game, in this chapter, I will walk you through the mathematical aspects of decisions that can help guide decision making when your emotions may cloud your thoughts.

Let's use a real life example. With all of the examples in this book, we all recognize they will not perfectly emulate your particular experience. I chose a fairly simple scenario for this example. Your situation might be more complex, but my hope is that this will provide you with basic information and insight to help you start thinking about the prudent course of action for your situation.

Real-Life Example #1: The Smiths

The Smiths, clients of mine, raised their family in a small rural community. Over the last 20 years, their children have all moved into a larger city several hours away, so the Smiths wanted to retire and buy a modest home, a "home closer to grandkids, recitals, and ball games" to be exact. Neither of them like debt. Just like thousands of other retiree's, the big question they had was, "Should we have a mortgage on our home or pay it off out of Mr. Smith's retirement account at his retirement?"

I helped them consider the facts in a simple, ball-park-numbers, manner:

- Based on what they could sell their home for and buy a new home they were short around $150,000. $150,000 to either finance or withdraw from retirement. Even if they were staying in the same house and still owed $150,000 on their mortgage, the following math would be applicable.
- Like nearly all of today's mortgages, they had a great low interest rate. After all, that is what triggered this whole planning scenario. If mortgage rates today were crazy high

like in the 70's and early 80's when the Smith's, and many of you, were buying a home, using a mortgage wouldn't even be a consideration.

- Based on their credit and interest rate, a $150,000 loan required a $630 per month payment, or $7,560 per year. When comparing the math, it is most accurate to leave taxes and insurance out of the equation. You are going to be paying those whether you have a mortgage or not.
- A $150,000 retirement withdrawal would be taxable, could make their social security more taxable, and would also make their Medicare costs go up. The actual withdrawal, plus the estimated tax cost for them, would be $200,000.

Part of their retirement strategy was to put $500,000 into a Guaranteed Lifetime Withdrawal Benefit (GLWB). We'll go over what a GLWB is in a later chapter. For this example, all you need to know is that the GLWB provides a guaranteed annual retirement income that this couple will be receiving each year for life. The annual income could go up, but it will never go down. Like many retirees, they liked the security and consistency of this plan, as opposed to retirement income from a pure investment account where the annual retirement income might fluctuate. In this scenario the GLWB makes it very precise to compare using 401k money to pay off a mortgage. For planning purposes, because the GLWB monthly payment is secure and consistent, it is easy to juxtapose that payment to a monthly fixed mortgage payment.

Let's look at the math for the Smiths.

- The $500,000 GLWB created a base **$26,750/year** pre-tax retirement income payment for them
- If they were to take out just over $200,000 to eliminate the mortgage that would leave around $300,000 in the GLWB

- Which equated to receiving **$16,000/year** of GLWB income
- After accounting for some estimated tax, the difference annually is **$8,960 less** retirement income each year by paying off the mortgage
- However, by paying off the mortgage, the Smiths would no longer be paying $**7,560/year** towards their mortgage payment
- Taking the difference of **$8,960 and $7,560**, by keeping retirement funds invested in a secure income source and **having** a mortgage the Smiths could increase their net retirement income by around **$1,400/year**

Being able to look at the numbers is a helpful place to start a conversation. But the math should not necessarily have the last word. Although the math indicates that the Smiths could come out ahead financially each year by using a mortgage, the Smith's desired not to have one. I suggested they go ahead and pay off their mortgage. My thinking was that the emotional benefits of not having a mortgage outweighed the $1,400 a year they would be getting. That made sense based on the goals and values that the Smiths had shared with me. Notably, once the Smiths sat down with the numbers, they did not see it as giving up $1,400 a year for peace of mind, they saw it as $1,400 a year less they had to spend on their grandkids. Camping, Disneyland, overnighters with the grandkids—these were some of their most important values. They opted to leave his retirement account invested to generate retirement income, use most of the income to cover the mortgage payment, and dedicated the surplus to spend on fun with their grandchildren. Once we put some actual numbers to the planning, we were able to more easily identify their strongest emotional drivers and their true priorities when it came to planning for retirement. For the Smiths, having their mortgage covered by a secure retirement payment fulfilled their need for security. Plus, having the extra money to spend on experiences with the grandkids, outweighed their desire to avoid a mortgage.

I encourage you to think about what your core values are. What's important to you about money? What do you want to do for yourself, your spouse, your children, grandchildren, and your community? There's no right or wrong here. What are your goals for retirement, and which of those goals have a higher priority?

When planning for retirement, facts and numbers can help initiate your decisions, but the emotional factors are also very important as they help dictate how you'll feel each day throughout retirement. It's imperative that you identify what factors are most

---

When planning for retirement, facts and numbers can help initiate your decisions, but the emotional factors are also very important as they help dictate how you'll feel each day throughout retirement.

---

important to you, so you can make the best decisions for your future. Remember, the best thing for you won't look the same as what is the best for someone else (even if that someone else sounds really smart talking around the water cooler at work). Don't be afraid to recognize your emotional goals, translate them into your core values, and let them help inform your financial decisions. That's not drama, that's a smart move.

By the way… another smart move is reading this book! Next up, Fed Funds and the National Debt.

Chapter 4

The Thirty-Trillion-Ton Elephant

Another big question pressing on people's minds is, "How long will interest rates stay low?" This affects people considering a refinance, retirees trying to live on interest, and a dozen other significant aspects of our lives. In the upcoming chapters, I am going to help you navigate the impact a low Federal Funds rate has on the economy, your savings, your mortgage, your investments and your overall retirement strategies. If low rates were going away tomorrow it would create a different set of circumstances, challenges, and opportunities. Conversely, I want to share some thoughts on why I think lower Federal rates are here to stay for a while.

In 2009 and 2010, I attended three conferences and heard from seven well-respected economists who all said confidently that within six to 18 months the FOMC would start increasing rates. Well, their timing turned out to be a little off—like eight years off! How could they be so wrong?

They were basing their theories on an old precedent, something we all have a strong tendency to do. Let me walk you through some numbers to help you understand the new precedent. I'll use numbers from President Obama's era because it corresponds closely to the FOMC's current policy stance. However, please note President's Trump's and Biden's National Debt numbers are right in line, or even higher. When it comes to racking up the National Debt, there does not seem to be a partisan distinction. It is a stark reality facing the American people—especially those who would like to retire or stay retired. Here are the round numbers:

In 2008, the National Debt was $10 trillion.

The yearly interest payment on that debt was $253 billion.

By the end of 2009, President Obama was on his way to becoming the president who would oversee the creation of the most National Debt ever. (At least, until he was surpassed in 2020 by President Trump. And now all odds are on Biden taking the cake.)

In 2009 the National Debt grew to $12 trillion. We all said, "Two trillion! In one year! Really?"

Can you imagine how high the interest payment was in 2009?

The National Debt went up by two trillion dollars in one year. Any guesses how much higher the interest payment went?

IT WENT DOWN—the interest payment on the National Debt went down to $197 billion!

To finish out the Obama-era numbers:

By 2012 the National Debt would be at $16 trillion.

By 2015 the National Debt doubled from the 2007 pre-recession debt level.

Yet the interest payment in 2015 was under $250 billion. That is lower than in 2008 when the debt was at $10 trillion and the interest payment was at $253 billion.

The National Debt had doubled, and the interest payment had gone down!

How is this even possible?

The answer is: Interest rates went down.

Talk about addictive. In this scenario the Federal government seems to get the best of both worlds: more money to spend and less interest to pay. This was a watershed moment for interest rates and monetary policy. As mentioned earlier, the FOMC traditionally managed slow economies by lowering interest rates from normal levels. This follows the theory that lowering rates makes money more accessible to businesses and individuals in order to stimulate the economy. Then, the FOMC would raise interest rates back up to curb inflation and to be ready for the next go around.

That dynamic appears to be long gone. Instead, the new normal is for Congress to influence the economy with stimulus programs, and issue debt to pay for it. You saw this in 2008–2009, then 2020, then again in 2021 and onward. The response from D.C. seems to be, "Why not?" The interest on the debt is at all-time lows. The Federal Funds rate's current target is 0%–0.25%. That Fed Funds rate basically sets the short-term National Debt rates and strongly influences the long-term National Debt rates. Congress and the president create stimulus bills and then put pressure on the FOMC to keep rates low. The second part of that equation is what the economists in 2009 were missing. They were using an old model where the FOMC was much more independent. The FOMC would lower rates as the economy cooled and raise them as the economy got too hot. Now, however, Congress passing and the presidents signing stimulus money has changed the model. They have placed themselves right in the middle of the FOMC's strategy. The FOMC cannot raise interest rates without dramatically cutting into the Federal budget.

With enticingly low interest rates, the National Debt has grown and will soon surpass $30 trillion. The National Debt is one big elephant in the economic room. And it is sitting on interest rates.

At low interest rates, even though debt continues to explode, it takes 7% to 10% of the Federal budget to cover the interest payments. With enticingly low interest rates, the National Debt has grown and will soon surpass $30 trillion. The National Debt is one big elephant in the economic room. And it is sitting on interest rates. We're at a point where any increase in interest rates would have a substantial increase in National Debt interest payments. Interest payments have to come out of the Federal budget. This will increase taxes and divert funds that are otherwise budgeted for Social Security, Medicare, Medicaid, defense, etc.

That's one of the big reasons I don't see interest rates increasing to a normal historical average anytime soon. Nobody in government wants to pay interest on all that debt at any higher interest rates. This puts tremendous pressure on the FOMC to keep rates low. It is also a game changer for you and your financial future. To create a secure plan, it will be important to understand how a low Fed Funds rate can affect the other rates that have an impact on the economy and on your money.

Chapter 5

Say Hello to LIBOR and Prime

No, those aren't the latest *Avengers* characters or a rock band from the 70s, they're two of the other interest rates you may need to pay attention to. Now that you are thinking about low Federal interest rates, you may be wondering what that has to do with the other interest rates out there. Up to this point, we've talked specifically about the Fed Funds rate in the U.S. But the big question we'll start to address is, "How does the Fed Funds rate influence the other rates that actually affect *you*?"

Today, the "rates" that people seem to hear, and ask me about, are:

- The Prime Rate
- LIBOR (pronounced "lie-bore")
- Mortgage rates
- CD rates and savings rates (such as Money Market Accounts or Bank Savings Accounts)
- Car loans

I will cover those areas over the next several chapters. Then, I'll get more and more specific on the major effects on retirement income rates. This will lead us into strategies for creating a secure retirement in a low-interest-rate world.

So, let's talk about LIBOR and Prime to get started. People seem to hear the phrases "LIBOR" and "the Prime Rate." I get questions about what they are. For many folks they won't have a direct impact on your retirement. However, they are two of the "rates" that it will be helpful to have a general knowledge of.

Let's start with LIBOR. LIBOR stands for London Interbank Offer Rate. It is published daily, so it can change daily. Because it's a daily average (technically called a "trimmed mean"), you can think of it as a daily average of how much the major global banks would charge other banks for a loan. LIBOR is really the only rate used world-wide and, one very distinct way it is different from the U.S. Fed Funds rate is that it is based on real loans being made in real time, as opposed to the Fed Funds rate that is set by the Federal Open Market Committee to manage monetary policy. There are certain variable rate loans that use LIBOR (instead of the U.S. Prime Rate) as a benchmark to adjust the interest owed on your loan. In general you will know if LIBOR affects you, because you'll know that you have a loan based on LIBOR.

Now, on to Prime.

As mentioned in Chapter 2, the FOMC meets eight times a year (or as necessary) to adjust the Fed Funds rate. Banks use this Fed Funds rate as the interest rate they charge other banks to make overnight loans to each other in order to maintain required bank reserves. Prime rate is based on, is slightly higher than, and moves with, the Fed Funds rate. Prime is the rate that commercial banks will offer to their most credit-worthy customers.

Simply put, LIBOR is global bank to bank loans, the Fed Funds rate is U.S. bank to bank loans, and Prime is U.S. banks to highest credit customer loans. Prime rate moves lock step with the Fed Funds rate—almost always exactly 3% above the Fed Funds rate. When the Fed Funds rate is .25%, Prime is 3.25%. LIBOR typically tracks the Fed Rate as well, but in times of global concern LIBOR can diverge substantially from Prime because the independent global banks make that decision on a day to day basis.

Prime rate will typically have a direct impact on lines of credit. Business's revolving lines and home equity lines of credit are some examples. Credit cards also fall into that revolving credit category. Revolving lines of credit loans are typically Prime plus some percent. The exact percentage is based on your credit and the loan-to-value ratio.

These two rates have decreased due to the lower Fed Funds rates. Fed Rates right now can't go any lower without going negative. So this could be something to take advantage of for now. Perhaps just as important is to avoid costly mistakes with these types of loans. There was a time when borrowers, typically business owners who were shopping loans, had grown accustomed to LIBOR as an alternative to Prime as their base rate. This type of loan could carry the added risk of an international disruption that could drive LIBOR higher, while the Fed Funds and Prime will likely be maintained lower.

I needed to touch on those two "rates" because they are well known, but now let's circle back to the rate that by definition is the closest to home.

Chapter 6

Mortgages, Treasuries, and the Fed

In this chapter, I'll answer the question, "How much are mortgage rates really affected by the Fed's actions?" The Answer is: a lot! As we talked about earlier, mortgage rates are very important as you decide the best way to pursue your retirement goals. Just as important as understanding mortgage rates, is recognizing the influence that the FOMC tactics are having simultaneously on *Treasury rates*, long term *National Debt interest*, and *mortgage rates*.

There are quite a few moving parts, so let's start with a quick review of some key components of what's involved:

The U.S. **Constitution** has a section granting Congress, with the approval of the president, the power to direct the secretary of the treasury to, "borrow money on the credit of the United States." (United States Constitution Article 8, Section 8, Clause 2)

Congress can spend more than it takes in and, with approval of the **president**, it can authorize the U.S. **Treasury** to issue debt to cover the expense.

The U.S. Treasury manages the funds of the U.S. government. This management includes collecting taxes, paying bills, and issuing what you and I call National Debt or Government Debt. The Treasury calls it "Public Debt" because the collateral backing this debt is the U.S. government's ability to tax you, me, and any businesses in the U.S. Fittingly, the U.S. Treasury is commissioned to collect taxes. To recap, the U.S. Treasury, as directed by Congress, can collect taxes, use it to pay government bills, and when the tax revenue is insufficient to cover spending, they issue National Debt called Treasuries.

Treasuries are issued by the U.S. Treasury in the form of:

- **Treasury bonds**
- **Treasury bills**
- **Treasury notes**

These bonds, bills, and notes (generically called Treasuries), are considered highly secure investments because they are backed by the U.S. government's ability to tax the largest economy in the world. When a person, bank, or financial institution buys U.S. Treasuries in the form of bonds, bills, and notes, that money goes to the U.S. Treasury. The U.S. government (Congress) directs the Treasury where to spend those funds. The Treasury bond investor (banks, pension funds, you, or me) has just loaned money to the U.S. government. The Treasury bond investor receives a promise to get back the amount they loaned the government at the end of the specified term. Plus, they get paid interest along the way.

If the government has just passed a large debt-funded stimulus package, the check you receive usually comes from the U.S. Treasury. That stimulus money was raised by the Treasury issuing National Debt (i.e. selling Treasuries to investors, like you, me, the Yale Endowment fund etc.).

Once the Treasuries are sold the first time (issued) they can then be bought and sold in the open market (traded), similar to the way Apple stock, or a General Electric bond, is traded in the open public markets every day.

When you buy, for example, a 10-year Treasury note it has an interest rate kind of like a savings account used to have a noticeable interest rate. There's a big difference though between a savings account and a 10-year Treasury. Savings accounts guarantee their same account value every day; the 10-year Treasury note guarantees the "account value" at the end of 10 years. Meanwhile, the "account value" of the Treasury note is going to fluctuate every day. On any given day you might be able to sell that Treasury note for more (at a premium) or less (at a discount) than you purchased it for. Which means that the new person buying the Treasury from you will likely be buying it at a discount or at a premium to the original (issue) price. I'll explain more about this concept later in this chapter.

The Federal Reserve Bank System is the Central banking system of the U.S. It was created in 1913 to supervise the nation's largest banks and provide financial services to the U.S. government. It is composed of 12 Federal Reserve Banks throughout the U.S.

- **The Federal Open Market Committee (FOMC)** is what the media calls **"The Fed."** It is the decision-making and policy-announcing public face of the Federal Reserve Banks. The FOMC regulates the U.S. economy in many ways.
- The FOMC sets and adjusts the amount that banks must keep on hand each day. This is called the bank's **Reserve Requirements**. Because the Federal Reserve is setting this Reserve Requirement, the funds held in the reserve are called **"Fed Funds."**
- A high Fed Funds Reserve Requirement is used to slow the economy. A low Fed Funds Reserve Requirement is intended to stimulate the economy.
- If a bank is short their Reserve Requirements, they borrow those funds from another bank or from the Federal Reserve at a "pre-set" Fed Funds interest rate. This pre-set interest

rate for bank-to-bank loans is the **Fed Funds rate** that we discussed previously in Chapters 2 and 4.

- The FOMC sets the Fed Funds rate—either low to encourage banks to loan freely, or high to persuade banks to be more tightfisted about handing out loans.
- The FOMC can also direct the Federal Reserve Banks to engage in **Quantitative Easing (QE)**. When the FOMC directs Federal Reserve Banks to buy Treasuries directly from the U.S. Treasury, or to buy Treasuries and other bonds in the open market it is called Quantitative Easing.
- Lastly, the Federal Reserve decides how much money there should be floating around in our economy. When it directs the Bureau of Engraving and Printing to print more paper bills, that is only to replace defaced or damaged bills.
- How the Federal Reserve really "prints money" in the way you and I would use the term is when it creates money electronically to purchase Treasuries and bonds as part of QE.
- When the Federal Reserve Banks buy a Treasury from you, me, a pension fund, or directly from the U.S. Treasury, it is real money that goes into our accounts. Even if the Fed just created it electronically out of thin air, we get the money in our accounts to use, reinvest, or cash out and go to the spa.
- By the same token, if Congress has instructed (and the president has approved) the U.S. Treasury to issue more National Debt to fund a stimulus package, the Federal Reserve Banks can electronically "print" the money to purchase treasuries from the U.S. Treasury. The newly created money used to purchase the treasuries is deposited into the U.S. Treasury account and Congress directs the U.S.

> Treasury how to spend it. The Federal Reserve Banks now hold the Treasuries purchased. They collect the interest payments on those until, at some point, they begin to sell them back into the open market.

Getting back to mortgage rates: One reason the FOMC uses QE is because the Fed Funds rate does not directly influence fixed mortgage rates. 15- and 30-year mortgage rates closely correlate to the yield of 10-year Treasuries—not the Fed Funds rate.

The following chart shows 30-year mortgage rates and the Fed Funds rates for January 2000 through March 2015. Notice that they are not overly correlated. For instance, find August 2007 to October 2008 on the chart. Look at the Fed Funds rate (dashed line). At that point, the FOMC had dropped the Fed funds rate from over 5% to 0%. That's a huge reduction. Yet, the 30-year mortgage rate barely moves from 6% to 5%.

Next, notice that in 2012 and 2013 mortgage rates finally dropped into the 3% range. This is not in response to the Fed Funds rate. The Fed Funds rate had been at 0% for four-plus years. In 2012 and 2013 is when the FOMC recommitted to Quantitative Easing. I will explain Quantitative Easing in detail momentarily. First, just notice that lowering the Fed Funds rate alone does NOT drive mortgage rates drastically down.

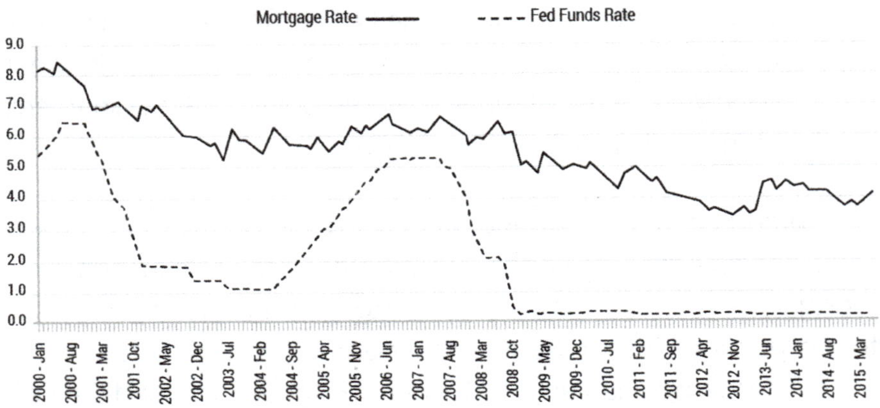

Sources: Freddie Mac(C), Federal Reserve

So how does the FOMC influence mortgage rates? The answer is:

- The FOMC directs the Federal Reserve Banks to engage in Quantitative Easing (buying *a lot* of Treasuries and mortgage bonds). The Federal Reserve currently has unlimited power to electronically "print" the dollars to do that.
- When the FOMC directs the Federal Reserve Banks to buy Treasuries, especially 10-year Treasury notes, the yield on 10-year Treasuries goes down.
- Fixed mortgage rates are closely tied to 10-year Treasury yields. So, if Treasury yields go down so will mortgage rates. Check out this next chart to easily see the 10-year Treasury yield and the 30-year mortgage rate correlation. Then I will explain how the Fed buying lots of Treasuries reduces Treasury yields.

When the FOMC directs the Federal Reserve Banks to buy Treasuries, especially 10-year Treasury notes, the yield on 10-year Treasuries goes down.

10-year Treasury yields and 30-year fixed mortgage rates (%)

The two rates track each other closely, suggesting common drivers.

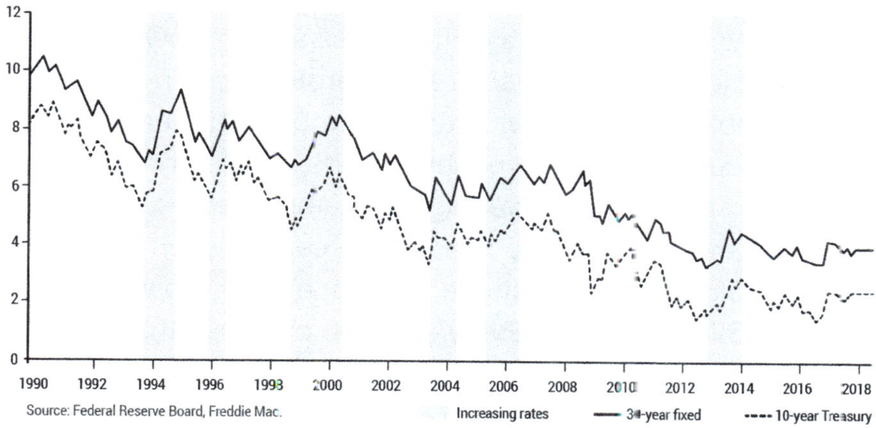

Source: Federal Reserve Board, Freddie Mac.

It is pretty easy to see the strong relationship between the 10-year Treasury yield and 30-year fixed mortgage rates. They move in tandem, with long term mortgage rates consistently 2% higher than 10-year Treasury yields. If Treasury rates go lower, then mortgage bonds can lower their rates and still be enticing to investors. If Treasury rates go higher, mortgage rates will move up. This is because no investor is going to buy a mortgage bond for the same yield as a Treasury. The mortgage bond is backed by folks like you and me paying a mortgage. The Treasury is backed by the U.S. government's ability to tax. The mortgage bond has more default risk, so investors that buy mortgage bonds will only do it if they get paid a higher interest rate for the added risk. That's why mortgage rates move up lock-step with Treasuries. Most applicable to the current environment, if Treasury rates go lower, then mortgage bonds can simultaneously lower their rates and still be enticing to investors.

The Treasury yield is the important part, because that's where mortgage rates correspond.

If the Fed can move Treasury yields down, then mortgage rates will go down in sync. So how does the Fed move Treasury yields down? They buy lots of Treasuries as part of QE.

It is time to explain *interest rate* **versus** *yield*. The Treasury Department sets the initial interest rate on a 10-year Treasury Note at issue. The *dollar amount* of interest paid on the note will stay consistent for all 10 years. For example, let's say you purchased a Treasury note, from the U.S. Treasury, when first issued for $1,000 at a 2% interest rate. After one year, you would have received $20 in interest. Every year the owner of that Treasury note gets $20 in interest. In investment-geek jargon the interest you get each year is called a "coupon," because back in the day of paper bond certificates, you had to cut a tab (coupon) off the edge of the certificate, and turn it in each year to get your interest payment. Hence, holding a note long term to collect the interest is called "clipping coupons". In our electronic day and age, the $20 of interest gets added to your investment account automatically, like any other interest earned. So, let's call the interest you receive the interest rate.

Now let's transition to yield. Yield is what you get when any Treasury gets resold in the open market at a price that is higher (premium) or lower (discount) than the original "issue price." Going back to my example of the Treasury you bought at issue for $1,000 that earns $20 a year of interest. If you sold that bond in the open market at a premium for $2,000, the purchaser would still only get the $20 per year in interest, because that was how it was issued. This would make the new investor's return on investment only 1%. That 1% is called yield. That is what this bond "yields" in interest to the new owner. On the other hand, if this Treasury is sold at a discount in the open market for $500, the new owner would be getting a 4% yield, as they would still be getting the $20 a year. The percentage return based on the purchase price in the open market is called the yield. If Treasury note prices never changed in the open market, then the yield would always match the initial interest rate.

The reality is that Treasury prices can change every minute of every day in the open market.

Unlike the old-days when you bought a Treasury note, received a paper certificate, and "clipped your coupons" for 10 years. Today, trillions of dollars of Treasuries trade every day on the open market. The open market is a really big auction. If there are a lot of buyers (or one huge buyer like the Fed when engaged in QE) the price of the Treasuries in the market will get bid up. Just like in my example from the last paragraph, when the prices of bonds are all at a premium because their price has been bid-up, the yield on those bonds goes down.

When the Fed enters the open market with billions and trillions to buy Treasuries, the price of Treasuries gets bid up really quickly. And the yield on Treasuries drops substantially. If yields on *open market* Treasuries are low, then the U.S. Treasury will set interest rates on *new issues* low as well. New issue Treasuries have to compete with the current yield of open market Treasuries. If open market Treasuries have low yields, the Treasury can set interest rates low on new issues. As addressed in Chapter 4, this keeps interest payment low on National Debt that is being created to pay for over-budget spending or stimulus packages.

If the FOMC wants to keep Treasury and mortgage rates low, then directing Federal Reserve Banks to buy lots of Treasuries is one way for the FOMC to accomplish that specific goal.

The Federal Reserve can also buy mortgage bonds, not just Treasuries, in the open market to greatly multiply the effect. The Fed buying lots of mortgage bonds in the open market bids up mortgage bond prices and drives the yield on mortgage bonds down. New mortgages, and refinance loans, can then be issued at lower rates and still be attractive to investors.

This action of buying Treasuries and Mortgage bonds is the major component of Quantitative Easing. QE is something the financial news talked about between 2010 and 2014. Remember the first chart in the chapter, it wasn't until 2012 and 2013 that mortgage rates dropped into the 3% range. This mortgage rate decrease was in response to QE. In 2012 the FOMC doubled-up on buying Treasuries and mortgage bonds. It was called QE3 if you recall that. The Fed increased their purchases to $45 billion a month of Treasuries and started purchasing $40 billion a month of mortgage bonds! This pushed mortgage rates to, up till then, all-time lows.

Hopefully you now have a better understanding of Quantitative Easing because it does not appear to be going away. In fact, the FOMC ramped QE up to unprecedented levels in response to COVID-related economic concerns. Mortgage rates dropped even lower than previous all-time lows. This monetary policy has major benefits from the FOMC's point of view. It keeps interest payments low on National Debt (Treasuries) and it keeps interest rates low for the typical consumer's largest debt (a mortgage). This approach by the FOMC can also make creating your retirement income more difficult.

For the foreseeable future, the FOMC has committed to purchasing Treasuries and mortgage bonds to support higher bond prices and, thus, keep Treasury yields and mortgage rates low. During the last recession, the FOMC kept the Fed Funds rate low and purchased bonds to keep yields low for eight-plus years. At some point, when the FOMC's directs the Federal Reserve Banks to start selling the Treasuries they have been buying, the yield on the 10-year Treasury will go up. That will be the time we could expect to see noticeable differences in mortgage rates. Based on the last recession, the FOMC will be very slow in their implementation of that.

Congratulate yourself.
There are a lot of moving parts to this concept.

Congratulate yourself. There are a lot of moving parts to this concept. You don't have to master it. Just know that you are beginning to understand some of the key rates in the economy and their correlation to the Fed's policies. Over the course of the next few chapters, we'll talk about auto loans, savings, CDs, pensions, and annuities as I help you develop knowledge and strategies needed to navigate this low-interest-rate environment.

First, a word on the rate of inflation.

Chapter 7

Inflation

When it comes to rates that the Fed policies influence, that in turn impact your finances, the rate of inflation is at the top of the list. The inflation rate is one of the most intrusive rates in our lives. Year over year, decade after decade, during your working years and especially during your retirement decades, the incessant increase in the cost of goods is a force to be reckoned with. In later chapters I will spend quite a bit of time explaining investments and strategies. Particularly, I'll cover those that can be helpful in combating inflation. For this chapter let's address what effect Fed policies will have on the inflation rate.

The Fed's purchases of Treasuries and bonds, as we have discussed, is possible because they can electronically create money. This is the modern day version of printing money. It's just less time consuming and no trees are needed for making paper. It can be immediate and practically unlimited. When the Fed enters into Quantitative Easing, the Treasuries and bonds it purchases are often held by large financial institutions and banks. The bank gets liquid money to add to their reserves. The Fed gets bonds or Treasuries added to their balance sheet. This flow of liquid funds to banks and financial institutions is anticipated to encourage them to loan money at convenient terms. This is a double edged sword because while extra funds could stimulate the economy, providing more jobs, production, and economic growth, more money chasing the same amount of goods can drive prices up That is inflation. There is currently a very reasonable concern about current and future inflation. This statistic should give you an idea of why this may be a significant concern. Following the 2008–2009 recession the Fed pumped $1.8 trillion dollars into the economy through QE over 5 years. In response to COVID, the Fed pumped $1.8 trillion into the economy through QE. Only this time they did that in five months. Not five years. Five months. That level of money created and injected in that short of an amount of time is causing a current spike in inflation and a very reasonable expectation of increased inflation going forward.

Another distinction between the QE that started in 2009 versus the QE that started in 2020 is how much the banks are retaining. When the Fed buys assets, cash floods into large banks and financial institutions, but what happens if the banks don't lend? What happens if the banks just stockpile the cash and add to their excess reserves? Well, we know what happens. Because that is what banks did in the 2009–2015 QE. During that time the banks' reserves rose simultaneously with the Fed's balance sheet assets. With the start of QE in 2009 and then their doubling up on QE in 2012 there were major concerns in the financial world of inflation or even hyperinflation. Yet, it did not materialize. The banks just "banked" their excess reserves and we had low to moderately low inflation.

This time around appears to be different. Banks have been lending enough that their excess reserves have been trending down. The Fed is also doing a lot of purchases directly from the Treasury, to allow Congress and the president to decide how this money will be spent. So while the Fed is practically doubling its balance sheet to well above $7 trillion, banks' reserves are trending down. When the gap between banks' reserves and the Fed's balance sheet widens, look for inflation to increase. 2021 already demonstrated hyperinflation in some elements of the economy (lumber for example). This does not seem to point, necessarily, to a long-term hyperinflation scenario. More likely, long term moderately high inflation is what we are facing.

There is one more important reason that I'm pretty confident that inflation will be running hotter in the future than it has in the last few decades: The chair of the Federal Open Market Committee told me. Technically he told you too. In his August 27, 2020 speech the chair of the FOMC, Jerome Powell, announced that a "revised consensus statement was adopted today with the unanimous support of Committee participants." Chair Powell's remarks can be found at www.federalreserve.gov/newsevents/speech/powell20200827a.htm.

He goes on to explain that, "Following periods when inflation has been running below 2%" like it had been, "appropriate monetary policy will likely aim to achieve inflation moderately above 2% for some time." This may look like a small percentage, but it is a substantial adjustment. The FOMC had previously been very quick to respond with higher rates to any signs of higher inflation. We'll touch on this again when we talk about Treasury Inflation Protected Securities in a future chapter because this revision to Fed Policy is a game changer. I don't think it is an overnight game change. I think it will be long term. It will have an effect during the decades of your retirement. Retirement is a time when finances are most vulnerable to inflation. The new approach by the Fed is that because inflation has been low, now they will let it run higher, and we'll get a "desired" long term average. As for how long and how high above 2% the Fed will allow inflation to run, the Fed is leaving that open-ended: "We are not tying ourselves to a particular mathematical formula that defines the average. Thus, our approach could be viewed as a flexible form of average inflation targeting."

Simply put, to create a secure retirement income you will need to address potentially higher inflation over a long period of time. We have spent time together understanding the Fed Funds rate, Treasuries, Quantitative Easing, and mortgage rates. I will address several other rates and spend quite a bit of time on potential solutions and strategies. Moving forward, the main theme will not only be the knowledge and strategies to address an extended period of low interest rates. The new reality is actually a bit tougher than that. The new goal is achieving a high-quality retirement in a low-interest-rate AND a potentially higher-inflation-rate environment.

The new reality is actually a bit tougher than that. The new goal is achieving a high-quality retirement in a low-interest-rate AND a potentially higher-inflation-rate environment.

Chapter 8

Auto Loans

After that discouraging chapter on inflation, let's talk about something more inspiring. How about: A new car! Okay maybe that's not your go-to inspiration, but I did promise that I would try to go through the various rates that might be a part of your financial life. I have started to touch on the correlation between the Fed Funds rate and all the other rates that impact your finances. In this chapter, let's quickly go over car loans and how they factor in.

Car loans are pretty straight forward. They are influenced heavily by the prime rate. As you may recall, the Prime rate is the rate that commercial banks will offer to their most creditworthy customers, and the prime rate moves lock step with the Fed Funds rate—almost always 3% above the Fed Funds rate. So the car loan looks at the prime rate and then is adjusted based on your credit.

For example, with a Fed Funds rate at 0% to .25%, the prime rate is 3.25%, the average new car loans are around 3.6% interest with a credit score over 750 and about 5% with a credit score in the high 600s. The lower the credit score the higher the rate.

One thing to note is that the rates a dealership offers versus the rates offered by a bank or a credit union are going to differ. For example, credit unions are technically owned by their members, so they follow rules to stay exempt from income taxes. Because of their business structure, a credit union can be tax exempt from a 21% corporate tax rate, meaning they can charge a lower rate for their loans. A for-profit bank, in contrast, has to build in profit and pay taxes, so they will likely have higher rates.

You'll often see credit union car loan rates that are close to or even at the prime rate. Credit unions are a worthy consideration for auto loans, and mortgages. Credit unions have a tendency of trying to muddle in other areas of finance that require specialized expertise such as estate planning, retirement accounts, and life insurance. I have seen that not turn out well. But for an auto or recreation vehicle loan, I have seen Credit Unions be really, really, competitive.

Allow me to be a bit sarcastic here: There's nothing better than extending your payments on a depreciating asset!

Car loan rates have come down and there are even refinance auto loans available which are lower, pretty much across the board, than previous rates. This concept seems a little counter-intuitive to me. Allow me to be a bit sarcastic here: There's nothing better than extending your payments on a depreciating asset! However, even as I say that, there is a time and place for refinancing your vehicle. The reality is that on a $50,000 car or on an $80,000 truck, a refi could make sense. Taken in connection with the broader context of retirement planning, the math could work in favor of an auto loan or refinance. For instance, Social Security and Pensions (specifically pensions that don't have a lump sum option) are going to pay a monthly allotment and nothing more. If all of, or most of, your income in retirement is coming from these types of lifetime fixed monthly payment sources, then financing vehicles could make sense. This will likely be a bit of a transition psychologically. In case my earlier comment wasn't proof, my personal bias is toward paying off assets that depreciate, and making ongoing "payments" or contributions to assets that have the potential to appreciate. This type of thinking puts more value on maximizing future income security. However, if your income consists of lifetime guaranteed payments, like Social

Security, Guaranteed Lifetime Withdrawal Benefits, pensions, and annuities, then your situation likely puts more value on maximizing current income. One way to maximize your income today is to pay off all your loans yesterday. If that didn't happen then refinancing to as low an interest rate, as long a loan period, and as low a payment as possible is another way to maximize current income. That strategy is where low-interest-rate vehicle loans could come into play for you.

One way to maximize your income today is to pay off all your loans yesterday. If that didn't happen then refinancing to as low an interest rate, as long a loan period, and as low a payment as possible is another way to maximize current income.

Speaking of annuities, in a few chapters I'll cover the effects that low interest rates will have on annuities and retirement accounts. Up next, let's cover savings, CDs, and fixed income rates. There is a lot to navigate in this low-interest, high-inflation-rate environment. I'll continue to give you the knowledge base you'll need for successful retirement planning.

Chapter 9

CDs and Savings Rates

We've talked a lot about the Fed Funds rate, which is set by the Federal Open Market Committee. Simultaneously we've addressed the 10-year Treasury Note—particularly the yield on 10-year Treasuries, and its correlation with long-term mortgages rate. So with that foundation in place, let's jump into Certificates of Deposit (CD) and Savings Account rates.

CD and Savings rates are affected by a combination of Treasury Rates, the Fed Funds rate and the supply and demand of consumers. Remember, the Fed Funds rates are the daily rates that determine what banks charge each other overnight, so it's an ultra-short-term rate. It's very similar to how a savings account is liquid every day, with no early withdrawal penalty. In this next chart, look at March, 2020. In March 2020 is when the Fed Funds rate (ultra-liquid, very short term rate for banks) was set at .00% to .25% after two emergency rate cuts by the FOMC.

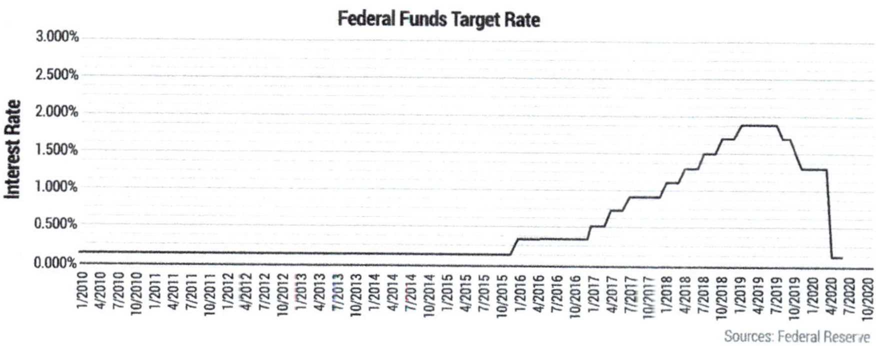

You can expect that savings accounts (also ultra-liquid, very short term rates for regular customers) are going to be in line with that. Following this Fed Funds rate decrease to 0% -.25%, the average rate on a savings account became .03% to .06%. This makes sense. It is right in line with the Fed Funds rate parameters. The two rates are very closely aligned, and are both so low that neither can go any lower without getting into negative interest rate territory.

Meanwhile, a "high interest" savings account might pay .05% to 1% higher than traditional saving accounts. They typically accomplish this little-bit-higher rate by a combination of:

- Being online, not brick and mortar
- Having a higher balance minimum (which, in turn, limits daily liquidity)
- Limiting transactions
- Often not providing debit cards.

All of these strategies are ways to minimize daily liquidity in order to pay a little higher rate. You can always cash out some or all of the account daily.

The important thing here is that having enough liquid funds is a fundamental aspect of your secure future. At this point, you and I both recognize that these funds are not going to be a growth asset. That's not their job. They are not going to keep pace with inflation. That's not their purpose. Your Emergency Fund, hopefully a decent chunk of funds, needs to be accessible. You don't want it to fluctuate, and preferably it should be FDIC or credit union insured. If you can get a better rate "online" and you are comfortable doing electronic transfers to the bank where you have your checking account, then that qualifies as accessible. You can take advantage of a little higher rate, and if you're ever in a financial pickle, then you can electronically transfer funds to your checking account and spend it on your needs.

Savings account interest is going to be way down for a long time when the Fed Funds rate is way down for a long time. Just plan on that. Coming up, I'll talk about some alternatives. Alternatives can be helpful to get a little more return, but in the end the important element of Emergency Fund holdings is not the rate. It's that it's there. With that in mind, savings accounts do provide accessibility and consistency for your Emergency Fund.

Next up: Certificate of Deposit (CD), Sometimes called a Timed Account.

CDs are interesting in that they are influenced by the Fed Funds rate and the 10-year Treasuries yield, depending on their term. Take a look at the following chart. It shows the Fed Funds rate and the six-month CD rate almost completely overlapping due to an obviously strong correlation between the two.

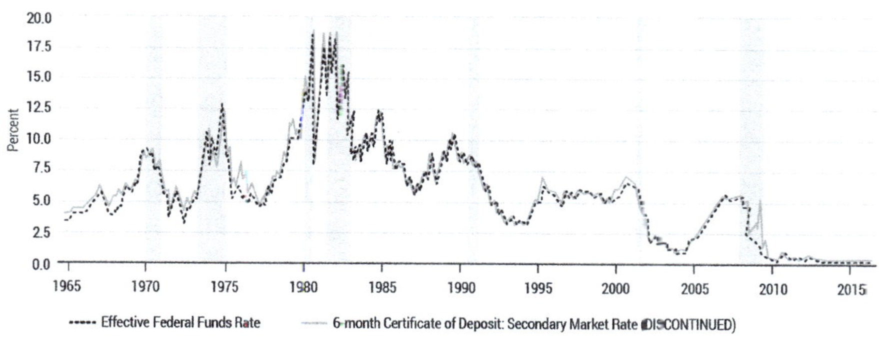

Sources: Bankrate.com, Federal Reserve

But as a CD gets longer in duration, its interest rate becomes less correlated to the Fed Funds rate.

In the next chart, you can see the Fed Funds rate and the average one-year CD rate. They follow similar paths, with peaks and valleys occurring at generally the same time, but there is disparity between the two. Take a look and then I will describe a few interesting take-aways.

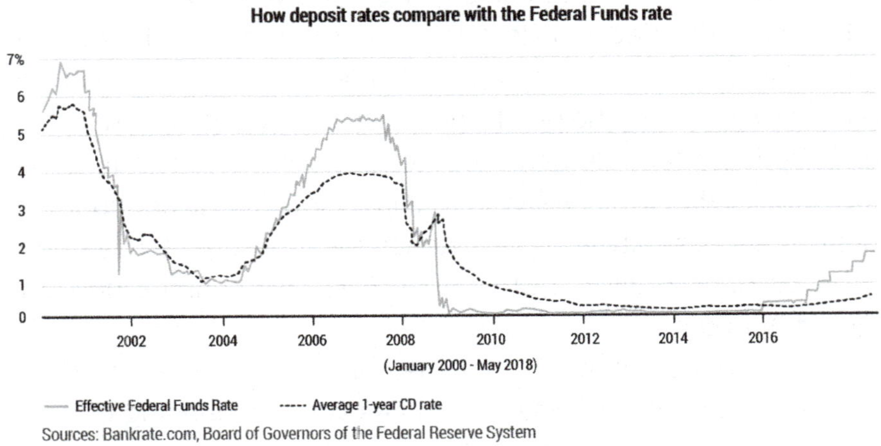

The longer duration a rate is for, the more it will deviate from the very short-term Fed Funds rate.

We are already in a low-interest-rate environment, so we will talk more about how to deal with that. But as a future planning strategy, it's important to take note of past trends. For example, in 2004–2005, CD rates actually started to rise first, as banks tried to attract more deposits in order to make more loans. Once the Fed started raising rates, the banks couldn't keep up. You can see the CD rates level off while the Fed Funds rate keeps climbing. Banks could not keep increasing CD rates and still be profitable. In addition, they didn't have to. Depositors felt like 3% on an FDIC account was pretty good. Meaning banks had plenty of deposits to meet their loan requirements, which meant bank CD rates lagged the Fed Funds rate during '06–'07.

Now, compare that to 2016 when, instead of the banks leading the way with rate increases, it was the FOMC who began increasing rates, and the bank CDs, on average, didn't respond that quickly. Which makes sense. If they have sufficient deposits to satisfy their requirements to make the loans they want to, and those deposits are locked in for one to five years at a low-interest-rate CD—meaning low cost to the bank—why would the bank be in a hurry to raise their rates and pay more for a new depositor that is going to cost them a higher CD rate for the next one to five years?

High interest savings accounts, on the other hand, do not lock in for a term, so they moved up with short term rates. During 2016, the upper echelons of high interest savings accounts were paying about 1.2% to 2.2% as the Fed Funds rate stepped up. At the same time, the one-year CD rates were averaging half a percent. That was a fascinating time for a finance geek. It could be applicable to you in the future.

Be conscious of these trends. Watch any Fed indications of moving out of the cellar and coming up to the basement. At that point, (possibly a ways down the road) if you want to maximize your yield on FDIC accounts, a high interest savings instead of a one- or two-year CD might be a better option.

You may still get 1% to 1.5% if you elect to do a five-year CD, because banks now need to outpace, not the short term Fed Rate, but 10-year Treasury yields to make their CDs attractive. However, I look at five-year CDs in two ways

First, if you have a five-year CD and you need to use the money before the five years is up, then you'll typically pay a penalty that equals 12 months of interest. This is not the end of the world, the reason you have it in the CD is for liquidity, accessibility, and FDIC insurance. If you're "never" going to touch that money, then you could simply put it in a growth allocation and forget about it. Not a CD. Alternatively you could use a five-year fixed annuity and get 2% to 4%. Not a CD. If you're going to be terrified of the CD penalty, don't use a CD. If we are talking about using CDs, we're talking emergency fund money—stable, liquid, and accessible. Meaning it is fine to access it even during the penalty period.

If you're getting 1% on $40,000, you would earn $400 a year. After a year, you could take it out, pay the penalty and still break even. At the end of the second year, you could take it out and keep an extra $400. Looking at it from this perspective, $400 on $40,000 thousand is still half a percent per year. That's better than savings at .06%, so don't get caught up on the CD early withdrawal penalty.

It's time for another soapbox moment: People will pay taxes and penalties on IRA withdrawals, or interest on credit cards or appliance loans, give up their right arm, and die on the sword to avoid paying an early withdrawal payment on their Emergency Fund CD. Don't get caught in that trap. CDs are great for your emergency fund, just don't forget that it's your *emergency* fund. A five-year CD is certainly not an accumulation vehicle in this low-interest-rate environment so don't treat it like it is. Treat it as a means to get a little more interest on your emergency savings. If you don't have an emergency you'll be that much further ahead on your interest. If you need to access it and pay a penalty it is just fine.

People will pay taxes and penalties on IRA withdrawals, or interest on credit cards or appliance loans, give up their right arm, and die on the sword to avoid paying an early withdrawal payment on their Emergency Fund CD. Don't get caught in that trap.

Second, if you and I are brainstorming options, and we are looking at a five-year CD, we likely need to get more clarity on the objective and time frame of those funds. Let's say you are heading into retirement and you have saved $100,000 in savings. These are funds that you now want to try and get some yield from while still keeping them liquid and accessible.

Let's determine how much of the money you want to be a true-blue emergency fund. Meaning, how much you would need to keep in accessible FDIC insured accounts, with no fluctuations. Then decide how much of the money is going to be more like reserve money, money you likely won't need for several years. You will likely know a few months or even years before making a big expenditure or taking a big trip. These "reserve account" funds we still want to keep liquid and easily accessible. They don't have to be FDIC insured.

Based on that, let's pretend that forty thousand is true-blue emergency fund money and you use a high interest savings account, linked to your checking account for quick accessibility, for that piece. Once the FDIC needs are fulfilled, then you can explore some investment options, other than a 5 year CD, that pay a higher yield while still being liquid, accessible and conservative, even if they fluctuate in value from day to day.

There are some good strategies for the reserve account allocations. We'll cover those in the next chapters. An important planning takeaway for a low-interest-rate environment is to increase the interest you are getting by dividing your Savings into FDIC insured Emergency Fund and a conservative, but not FDIC-insured Reserve Account. Great rates on CDs and Savings Accounts are not happening. Instead, by dialing in the goal, objective, and time frame of your "Savings," you'll be able to pair an allocation to true-blue savings Emergency Fund accounts with an allocation to alternatives that are extra reserves. By doing this you can construct an overall higher yield. As you get the goals of your funds nailed down, everything else will start to fall into place. You can plan for an emergency while still being smart about preparing for the future.

Chapter 10

Short-Term Bonds

As we leave FDIC-insured Savings and try to get a little more interest on your "Reserve Accounts," there are a few options. What will work best is dependent on your personal situation. If you have two to three months of income in your total savings, that probably needs to be FDIC-insured Emergency Funds. However, if you have over six months income in your savings and you have a little longer time frame, then keeping it all in low-interest FDIC-insured accounts might not make sense. In this chapter I'll go over short-term bonds. This is one alternative to savings accounts and CDs for money that is in addition to your desired Emergency Fund holdings.

At this point you are much more informed than most people. Moving forward, my intention is to continue explaining how different types of investments are affected by low interest rates, and correspondingly I will give you some sound and simple ideas on how to utilize these different holdings to accomplish your goals. I voluntarily became a fiduciary to my clients years ago because the work is pretty straight forward in my mind—just do what's right for each person. Since I don't know your individual situations, I hope to provide you with the information you'll need to make informed decisions. To do that, my approach is to cover the various investments, products, and indexes simply and also provide implementable knowledge to help you take charge of your future.

A conservative alternative to an FDIC Savings or CD account that is worth exploring is short term bonds. Long, medium, and short term bonds are also called fixed income. With these types of holdings, we have left the FDIC world so the account value of the investment will fluctuate. If interest rates change, so will the value of a bond. The textbook explanation of a bond's movement in value is that of a lever and fulcrum, as interest rates go up, the value of a bond goes down in the open market. What's important to focus on is Interest Rate Risk, or more specifically, Interest Rate Sensitivity. Interest rate sensitivity is a measure of how much the value of the bond account is going to change when interest rates move.

So let's look at an example. Say I bought a bond last year for $1,000 that pays 4%. If I want to sell the bond tomorrow, instead of holding it all the way to bond maturity, the rate of new bonds in the market will make a big difference in the value I receive when I sell my bond. If people can buy new bonds for 4%, I can easily sell my bond for $1,000; but if new bonds are at 3% or lower, (like has happened since March of 2020), then I can sell my bond for more. But if new bonds are paying 5%, no one will be willing to buy my bond for $1,000, so I'll get less than that if I sell it. How much less will depend on the term length of the bond. Like a lever, the longer-term bond you have, the greater its value will fluctuate when interest rates change.

Following is a basic chart that illustrates the general effects of duration (think of duration as: the term length of the bond) and a 1% interest rate change. The chart shows how an interest rate *increase* of 1% forces *down* the value of a six-year bond about 6%. The same 1% increase in interest rates drives the two-year bond down 2%, and it has *even less* (if any) impact on the ultra-short duration bond.

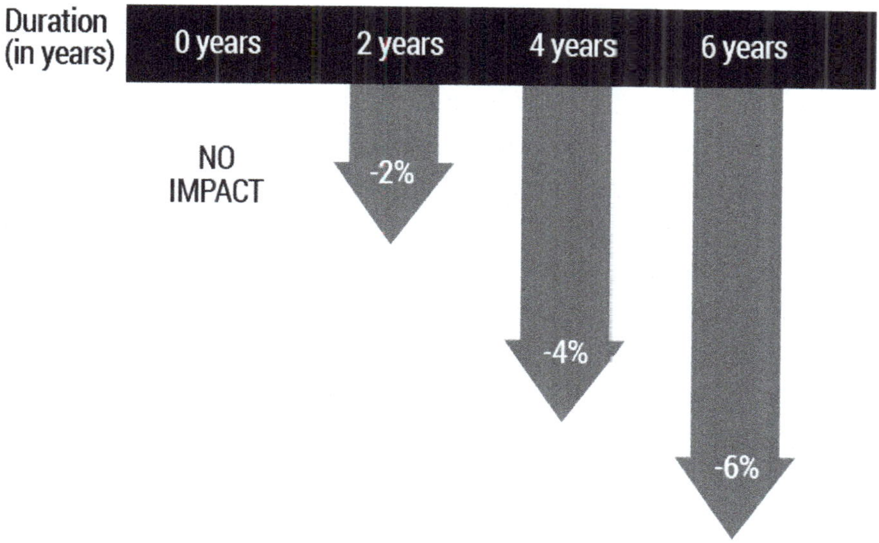

This chart doesn't even include 10, 15, or 30-year bonds but the trend continues. Longer term bonds have substantially higher interest rate sensitivity. This means, as interest rates rise, longer term bonds will decrease significantly more in value than short and ultra-short duration bonds.

One interesting thing to note is that current interest rates (hopefully) can only go up. It might be a while before that happens. When it does happen, your finances could look ugly if you're in long-term, interest rate sensitive bond holdings.

So how can you navigate this low-interest-rate environment with emergency fund and reserve account money? For the true-blue emergency fund money, I lean toward using FDIC insured accounts—like money market and high-interest savings accounts. For the reserve portion that you still want to be liquid, accessible, and pretty conservative, there are a few different options. Remember this reserve is your second line of defense protecting your retirement. It's the buffer between your retirement assets and life. So even as you try to get a little more interest, keep it accessible and conservative.

Before understanding interest rate sensitivity and the risk associated with that, you might have been tempted to go for a longer duration bond holding because you can get 4%–5% yield from that. That can make sense if you're comfortable with the potentially larger fluctuations of your account value. For reserve account money, you might consider short term, short duration or ultra-short bonds. Ultra-short bonds are often used to try to get an additional 1% or maybe 2% above what you can get in CDs, high interest savings, or money markets. These assets can have an important place in navigating this low-interest-rate environment. With the right amount of funds and the right time frame, incorporating short term bonds allocation can make sense.

Frankly speaking, run far away from anyone promising a greater return at no additional risk.

Let's talk about the additional risk for a minute. Frankly speaking, run far away from anyone promising a greater return at no additional risk. Ultra-short bond funds have more risk than CDs or Savings; it comes with the territory when you try to get a little higher yield. Namely, these bond funds are not FDIC-insured. In addition, not all short duration funds are the same, so be sure to review the underlying holdings of the fund. Now you are in a position to decide how much to allocate as your Emergency Fund (FDIC-insured) and how much will be your short duration Reserve (short duration bond funds). This is, as I've mentioned before, why planning successfully for retirement often comes down to accurately establishing your goals, priorities and time frame. I will give you an example in the next chapter of how the short-term money puzzle can fit together.

As you can tell, there's a lot to navigate in this low-interest-rate environment. Having one account with no risk and paying mountains of interest would be great in a high interest rate world. In a low-interest-rate world, it takes quite a bit more effort to assemble a secure solution. With the knowledge you're gaining and a clear picture of what you want your future to look like, you are on your way.

Next stop: Fixed Time Period Annuity

Chapter 11

Short-Term (Three- or Five-Year) Fixed Annuities

It can be tricky in low-interest environments to get interest on your short-term, needs-to-be-safe money. It was easy when an FDIC-insured money market paid 3.5%. You used to be able to say, "I might need it now or in a few years, either way I'll just stick it in a high-interest savings or money market account and I can get three or even four percent easy." (Ah, the good ol' days.) Unfortunately, that's no longer the case, and likely won't be anytime soon.

Now, in order to gain interest on these short-term funds, it takes a little more planning (and call me biased, but I love retirement planning!) You didn't realize this was going to be so much fun did you? Well, it's about to get even better. I'm going to teach you about annuities. Understanding annuities from a dispassionate perspective might be one of the best things you learn from this book. Let's have some straight talk about: the different kinds, how they work, when they might be a great fit, and when they're awful. I'll start with three-year to five-year fixed time period annuities.

Dialing in on how much of your money you want set aside as your Emergency Fund—ultra liquid with no fluctuation FDIC-insured—versus how much you want in a conservative Reserve Account—one- or three- or five-year money that you'd like to get a little interest on—is crucial for planning for your retirement. This is where a plain vanilla, fixed time period annuity might make sense.

For example, here are some generic fixed annuity rates from June of 2020—a very low-interest-rate period. A three-year annuity rate was 3% per year. A five-year annuity rate was 4.15% per year. This is compared to the current "high-interest" savings account rates we previously discussed at around 1% and the three-year CDs at around 1.5%. Then, as you move up the risk ladder to ultra-short bond funds (and remember to choose those with high quality holdings) the interest was around 2.5% per year. Finally, from there, you can look at the longer duration bond portfolios to try to get 4% per year. Due to interest rate risk on long-term bonds, let's drop those as an option for now.

When you start to compare those interest rates, you can see why something like a three-year annuity has a place in many people's holdings. They provide a specified rate, a short- to mid-range timeframe and no risk of fluctuations. Those are the benefits. What about the down side? Less accessibility. Let's address what they ARE and what they are NOT.

Fixed time annuities are a contract between the insurance company and you. The insurance company guarantees:

- The principal invested
- The rate of interest over a specified term

Fixed time period annuities are designed so that each dollar you put in goes to work for you by getting the specified interest rate during the specified time period. The principle and the interest rate guarantees are backed by the insurance company not by the FDIC.

Fixed time period annuities are designed so that each dollar you put in goes to work for you by getting the specified interest rate during the specified time period.

What these annuities are not is 100% accessible. They have a surrender schedule causing you to pay a penalty if you cash out before the end of the three-year or five-year time period. As a buffer against that, these types of investments will most often have provisions where you can take out a portion of the account without any penalty. The penalty-free amount that can be withdrawn during the surrender schedule period is typically either the interest earned or 10% per year of the account. With this baseline knowledge, you can double check the specific provisions so you understand how it works.

From this perspective, I'd suggest you treat the annuity as inaccessible money for that time period. Plan accordingly. If you think you likely won't be needing the money for a few years but there is still a chance you will need it, then stick with an ultra-short bond fund. Now let's expand the example to see where a three-year fixed annuity would be a good fit.

For instance, let's say you're going into retirement with a pension and social security as your monthly income. That's not quite enough to satisfy your retirement goals, so you allocate some of your 401k to strategies that generate additional secure monthly income (this is something we'll cover in glorious detail in later chapters.) At this point you have secure monthly income, so next you need to address setting up your short term secure funds.

As previously described, your Emergency Fund (FDIC insured) is for unexpected expenses and your Reserve Account (ultra-short term bonds) are additional funds that you want available just in case. It is so true in life that most often if you have the funds available, then you won't need them, but if you don't have accessible funds, you will end up needing them. The "disaster devil" seems to stay away when there's no room to play. It's quaint but true. That is why we are spending this amount of time trying to get just a little more interest on these short term secure funds. We want you to have them and preferably not have to use them. Hence, why we'd like to see you make a little interest on them.

Now that Emergency and Reserve funds are off to a solid start, you want to think about the goals you have other than avoiding disaster. Let's say the next two goals are vacations and service. You want to retire, visit family, take some expensive vacations, and relax for two or three years without having to worry. These trips will cost you more than the monthly budget you've prepared for so you'll want a fund earmarked for this purpose. Guess what kind of account I'd suggest you use.

It may be a trick question, but the answer is NOT a fixed time annuity, even though that's what this chapter's been building up to. In actuality, a fixed time annuity wouldn't be a great fit in this scenario because you'll need the liquidity and accessibility over a short time period of just a year or two years. I'd recommend going back to a high-interest savings account for these funds.

Remember, planning for retirement isn't just about numbers, it's about peace of mind and doing what brings you joy.

Okay, we've got your travel for the next few years covered with the high-interest savings, but you know after those first few years of travel, you want to dedicate yourself to a cause that's important to you. Remember, planning for retirement isn't just about numbers, it's about peace of mind and doing what brings you joy. Many of my clients have gone on extended service trips after they retire: church, humanitarian, and service missions. Education, historical, and health care initiatives. They often are gone for extended periods of time, several months or even for several years. These have been some of their best retirement experiences. Sometimes they have been able to afford these service trips out of their regular budgets, but more often, they wanted to have extra money set aside. They wanted funds allocated so that no matter the calling or the adventure, they could make it happen.

In our example, you know you want to pursue this in three years, and you'll want to dedicate a portion of your funds to making sure this can happen. You're not going to want the money sitting at low interest for three years and you don't want it fluctuating in the broader investment markets, so where does that leave you? You got it, we're now ready to look at a fixed time period annuity. With your money in a fixed time period annuity, you'll know exactly what you'll get out at the end of the period. Along the way you'll get more interest than in savings. These annuities can be perfect for mid-range planning and creating security in that part of your retirement plans.

The fixed time annuities are directly driven by your goals and values for retirement, so make sure you know those and begin applying your freshly gained knowledge to your retirement planning.

Chapter 12

Lifetime Payment Annuities

While we are on annuities, let's take three chapters and clear up some confusion. In the last chapter, I went over fixed time period annuities. You now know that these will typically have shorter time periods like three or five years. Fixed time period annuities are certainly not the only type of annuity out there; however, all annuities tend to get lumped together by various TV and radio financial talk show hosts. That is a disservice to retirees. In this chapter, I'm going to explore lifetime payment annuities, both what they are and how they have been impacted by the recent changes in interest rates.

One thing to keep in mind is what I'm NOT talking about in this chapter. To be clear, a lifetime payment annuity, or a fixed payment annuity, is NOT:

- A Variable Annuity
- An Equity Indexed Annuity

We'll cover both of these other types of annuities in later chapters, but this one is all about the lifetime payment annuity.

In my opinion lifetime payment annuities are pretty old school. When I was growing up in a little farming town, classic chevy trucks with the step-side were considered the coolest thing. There were some other cool things—like 4th of July water fights at the town park and floating down the Virgin River on an old patched-up tractor tube. Old Chevy step-sides were the coolest though. I still think those old trucks are fun, and they have value for sure, but

I have many clients now that pull toy haulers and recreation trailers all over the country as part of their retirement travel. As cool as I think old trucks are, I would not encourage my clients to buy a '57 Chev' with the step-side for their cross-country travels. Instead, there are modern vehicles that would be way better for their purposes. It is the same with retirement vehicles. Lifetime payment annuities may have been attractive in the past, but depending on your goals and retirement values, there are potentially much better options for these modern times.

As cool as I think old trucks are, I would not encourage my clients to buy a '57 Chev' with the step side for their cross-country travels. Instead, there are modern vehicles that would be way better for their purposes. It is the same with retirement vehicles.

For now, I think it's important to help you understand how a traditional lifetime payment (or Life-pay) annuity works so you can decide whether or not it is the best option for you. Some of you will still have this type of annuity as part of your retirement plan, maybe without even realizing it, so it's critical to understand what it is.

Here's how it works. You, or your employer, put your retirement money into the annuity and then either immediately, or at a specified time in the future, the contract will "annuitize." Annuitize means you start to get guaranteed payments every month. Those payments are guaranteed by the insurance company and will pay out for a guaranteed period. When that period is over there are no more payments. The period for these annuities is most often your life. It can be you and your spouse's lives (joint life). You could also elect to get a set payment for 10 years, or 20 years. You get to decide. One important concept is that the longer the payment is guaranteed for, the less the payment will be.

For example, a joint lifetime payment means that if you die then the payment continues to your spouse. Compared to a single lifetime payment, the joint lifetime payment will be lower because there's a high probability that you won't both die on the same day. A joint lifetime will statistically pay out longer than a single life. The longer the guaranteed payment the lower the monthly income. That's not to say that I'm opposed to joint lifetime payments. In fact I'm a huge proponent! Surprisingly, sometimes I have to strongly encourage one spouse to not leave their husband or wife high and dry, if they die first, just to get a higher income while both are alive. We all want to die together, no one (in a happy relationship) looks forward to life without their spouse, but we also know that there is a very high likelihood that one person will die several years before the other.

If you live long and use up all the funds you put into the annuity, the insurance company is on the hook to keep paying you. That's a plus! However, if you have a Life-pay annuity, and you die before you have received all of your funds, the annuity company keeps the remainder of the money. That's a major negative! Baby Boomers tell me they do not want that.

The next thing to consider is how these Life-pay annuities are affected by this low-interest-rate environment. Let's look at a real-life example. (As before, names are modified for security and numbers are rounded off for ease of calculation.)

Real-Life Example #2: The Joneses

Back in 2008, my clients, the Joneses wanted a portion of their TIAA account in a true-blue joint lifetime annuity. TIAA is a company that provides retirement plans for a lot of universities and hospitals (it stands for Teachers Insurance and Annuity Association of America). TIAA still has this older-style annuitization as an option. My clients needed and wanted around $2,600 a month of joint lifetime income, so they directed around $490,000 of their TIAA money toward the TIAA joint lifetime annuity. In comparison, if they had gone with a single life annuity that same dollar amount would have generated around $3,200 per month in income.

$2,600 versus $3,200.

You can see, in the Joneses' case there was about a 20% reduction in monthly income in order to cover two lives. You will need to build that into your planning. Now let's get back to the impact of low interest rates.

If the Joneses were setting up their retirement today in this low-interest-rate environment, as opposed to the higher interest rate environment they were in during early 2008, they would get less of a monthly lifetime payment. Using the same ages, dollar amounts, and other parameters, their monthly payment with a Single-Life-pay would be about $2,700 per month, compared to $3,200 in 2008. This $500 per month ($6,000 per year) reduction is a consequence of interest rates being lower. If you want to replicate the Jones's retirement income in today's low rate environment, you would have to put $581,000 into the annuity. That is compared to $490,000 in 2008. Goodbye $91,000 that you could have done something really fun with in retirement.

See what a game changing effect low interest rates have on retirement income.

On a related note, my team and I help a lot of clients retire from universities, colleges, and hospitals. As a firm, we have a focused expertise on helping educators and health care professionals. It is truly our passion to help bless those who have blessed society. Like the Jones', many other educators and healthcare professionals have their retirement accounts through TIAA or similar systems. These systems still have the option to annuitize old-school style, but they also have other options that are much more applicable to the current era.

Because we help our clients manage and make retirement decisions with their TIAA accounts, my team has witnessed, in real-time, a major shift in retirees' mentality over the last 10 years. The previous generation was pretty comfortable with the traditional annuity approach. Retirees were willing to take whatever retirement payment the company offered. Then, when they died, the company kept whatever funds were left unused in the retirement fund. For instance, the Federal Employees Retirement System and many state retirement systems are based on this older system. They do not offer lump sums, so your only option is to get a lifetime annuity payment. The downside is, once you start the payment, if you pass away the next day or in 20 years, your unused funds revert to the company. Previous generations were okay with that.

Baby Boomers on the other hand, are a different breed. I love you guys. You want a secure retirement income AND, if you die early, you want that unused money to go to your children or your favorite charity. This mentality has created the major shift we've seen. Fifteen years ago, clients took the lifetime payment. Now, almost unanimously, client's take a lump sum transferred into a retirement account, use those funds to create consistent retirement income, and preserve the ability to pass unused funds to beneficiaries.

Now that you understand how lifetime payment annuities work and are affected by low interest rates, although likely not the way you'll decide to go, you can make a decision with confidence.

Chapter 13

Indexed Annuities

Usually the way a client or prospective client asks about what I would call an Indexed Annuity is by saying something along the lines of, "I've heard about one of these deals where your account can grow like the stock market, but you never lose money which sounds good but a little far-fetched." There is typically a misconception around getting stock market-like returns (I'll explain why that's not quite accurate in a little bit), yet these questions act as a lead-in to a great educational conversation about an Indexed Annuity.

So, what is an Indexed Annuity?

First, there are a couple different names for indexed annuities. Agents that are only licensed to sell life insurance can only use "Fixed products" with their clients. They will often call them Fixed Indexed annuities, or FIAs. Advisors that have both an insurance license and investment licenses (called securities licenses) will often refer to them as Equity Indexed annuities or EIAs. Two names, same thing.

Second, every contract is going to have unique features, but there are a few general guidelines you should know:

- You'll want the money you put into an Indexed Annuity to be longer-term money because there is usually a seven- or 10-year surrender penalty period. During this time, if you surrender or "cash out" from the annuity there will be a penalty charged by the insurance company to offset their cost of establishing the contract. If you're going to cash out after a fairly short time, then this is not the right place for your funds. (We've explored much better options for shorter term money in previous chapters.) That's not to say you can't draw some money out each year. The contracts will usually let you take out 10% each year without triggering the surrender penalty—so there are some strategies that may work for your retirement plans. For example, you could skim off the interest each year, so you're taking out less than 10% each year. That amount will be surrender-penalty-free even during the surrender schedule period.

- The guarantees in an Indexed Annuity are an agreement or contract backed by the financial strength of the insurance company. It's not FDIC insured money, so you'll want to use an insurance company with a high financial strength rating.
- The insurance company guarantees the principle but the interest rate you receive is based on some type of crediting method. This crediting method is where the low-interest-rate environment can have a major influence.

Let's talk in general terms about crediting methods. Remember this is not a "fixed interest" annuity where the interest is set by the insurance company. Neither is it a Variable Annuity type where you have sub-accounts that are actually invested in stock and bond market allocations. You could think of an Indexed Annuity as "in between" those two. The money you invest in an index annuity goes into the general account of the insurance company and then, usually once a year, the insurance company credits interest to your account based on a crediting method.

The most basic types of crediting methods are called "participation rate" and "cap rate" ("cap" for short). I won't go into all the types of crediting methods (for example: monthly average, quarterly averages, multi-year cap, spreads, or performance triggers), just know that there are other crediting methods out there. If you have decided you are never going to invest in the stock or bond markets again and you feel ripped off by FDIC insured rates, then you will likely end up investing in an Indexed Annuity and that will be the time to explore different crediting methods. For now, let's just look at how a participation rate and cap rate can work.

The insurance company is going to give you a few market-based indexes to choose from. Your options will likely include indexes like the Russell 2000 Index, the S&P 500 Index or the Bloomberg-Barclays Aggregate Bond Index. In the upcoming chapters, I will be spending quite a bit of time explaining market indexes. I will explain the stocks that make up the Russell 2000 and the S&P 500, as well as the bonds that comprise the Barclays Aggregate Index. All of the knowledge you gain in those chapters about indexes will help you understand the index crediting investments that are available inside your Indexed Annuity. Don't stress about it right now. At the moment just know that each annuity will offer different indexes, or blends of multiple indexes, for you to choose from. For simplicity, let's say that you can choose a crediting method based on the S&P 500 Index. In this method you get to participate in *a portion of the gains* and *none of the losses* of that index. Let's look at a hypothetical of how interest would be credited to your account. Then I'll explain how the insurance company accomplished this.

Let's say an insurance company offers a participation rate of 70% or a cap of 5%, based on the returns of the S&P 500 stock index.

- Year 1: The S&P 500 index does 10% for the year. Your account stays flat during the year and on the anniversary date, if you did the 70% participation you get 7% added to your account value. Or if you'd elected the 5% cap you get 5% added to your account value.

- Year 2: The S&P 500 index has a 3% negative return. Your account gets a 0% return. You gave up some of your growth potential in the "good" year, in order to avoid losses in a "bad" year.
- Year 3: The S&P 500 index does 6% for the year. With the 70% participation option, you get 4% added to your account. Or with the 5% cap option you get 5% added to your account.

In this example the S&P 500's cumulative return over 3 years is 13% (+10, -3, +6 = 13%). The cumulative return of the participation crediting method is 11% (+7, 0, +4). The cumulative return of the cap crediting method is 10% (+5, 0, +5). An Indexed Annuity should not be expected to keep pace with the actual index over an extended period of time. That's not it's job. If you want to try to keep pace with the S&P 500 index, you would buy an index fund and go through all the ups and downs of the S&P 500 index. That pure-investment-index fund has a place that we will talk about in-depth during the latter portion of this book. For those of you that do not want to go through the losses in the markets, an Indexed Annuity can avoid all the negative years. That is its job. Avoiding negative years and having the opportunity to get more interest than fixed or FDIC-insured accounts is the goal with an Indexed Annuity.

Avoiding negative years and having the opportunity to get more interest than fixed or FDIC-insured accounts is the goal with an Indexed Annuity.

Some of you are wondering, "How do you participate in some of the *ups* of the markets and none of the *downs*?" Let me explain in generic terms how this crediting method works—especially because it helps us understand the impact of a low-interest-rate environment.

Let's say you decide to put some of your money into an Indexed Annuity. The funds you put into the Indexed Annuity will go into the insurance company's general account. Please note, the funds you put into an Indexed Annuity *do not* get invested into an index fund; your money goes into the insurance company's general account. There is a lot of money in an insurance company's general account. It's not just sitting there in cash. This money is invested in very long term, pretty secure bonds—like class A commercial building mortgages for example. Investments in the general account will pay ongoing interest into the general account. Each year some of the bonds in the insurance company's general account mature and have to be reinvested into new bonds. The insurance company uses some of the interest generated in their general account to buy options on whatever market index you decided to use in your Indexed Annuity. If the market-index goes down over the year, then those options expire worthless. That's why you get a 0% return for that year in your Indexed Annuity. If the index goes up, then the options deliver a gain for the year. The insurance company takes out enough of the gain to buy options for the next year. Then, your account gets credited with the remaining profits. That's why you get some, but not all, of the grains of the index.

When it comes to a low-interest-rate environment, here's where things really get interesting (and a tiny bit discouraging). When yields on treasuries and mortgages go down (Since you've learned about this you are probably thinking to yourself "Treasury yields go down when the Federal Reserve starts pumping money into the economy by buying Treasures and other bonds, this is also known as Quantitative Easing," Perfect! You nailed it! Fist Pump!) the bonds and mortgages purchased in the insurance company's general account will yield less interest.

Less *interest* in the general account means less money to buy *options* for your Indexed Annuity.

Fewer *options* means a lower *participation* in the index's gains.

Lower *participation* in the indexes gains equals lower *participation rates* in the annuity.

As salt in the wound, the reason the Fed is pumping money into the market is because the market is going through a lot of volatility. Volatility in the market causes *options* to be more *expensive*.

More expensive options equals *lower* caps in the annuity.

Now you can see why caps and participation rates on new contracts will be lower in a low-interest-rate environment.

That's all kind of a downer, but it is reality. Still, indexed annuities might have a place in your retirement as a way to reduce risk and increase returns on conservative assets. Their returns will likely outpace conservative bonds. Remember, bond prices can fluctuate down in value in any given month or year. Indexed annuities don't have any negative months or years. Please remember, they do have a seven- or 10-year surrender penalty schedule. Maximizing the return, minimizing the risk, and navigating low interest rates is always easier the longer you have to let a plan develop. That's why it is so important to get a plan in place or updated immediately to achieve and continue your successful retirement.

One big glimmer of hope is that investment product companies are listening. This generation of retirees is pretty worn out with the risk of the market and you want some security. Conversely, you are not happy with FDIC rates. You the consumers are driving insurance companies to make these products available. This competition for business in the market place is driving insurance companies to get more and more competitive with each other and creative in how they increase their crediting methods. That's something I really like to see because frankly, if the caps get high enough, who wouldn't be interested in benefiting from that? So if we go the Indexed Annuity route it's imperative to shop the gamut to find the right product for you and your retirement plans.

Speaking of finding the right product for your retirement goals, some of you are going to love the next chapter.

Chapter 14

Variable Annuities

This is the last chapter on annuities before I move on to teaching you all about pure-investment strategies. For some of you, this will be the most important chapter in the book. For others it might be your least favorite. Some of the most fun education that my team and I provide is teaching our clients about pure-investment accounts (with their pros and cons) compared to a Variable Annuity that has a Lifetime Withdrawal Benefit Guarantee and Death Benefit Guarantee (with its pros and cons). We are very comfortable utilizing either one or implementing a blend of the two. Consequently, after we teach the two concepts, we ask the client if they like one type of account more or less than the other type. The client responses are super meaningful. We have clients respond that they absolutely love the Variable Annuity with the guarantees and that finally they can sleep at night knowing their retirement is secure. They are so excited. Other clients tell us they appreciate the education, but they are totally comfortable with pure-investment accounts. The beautiful thing is that once you clearly understand the options, you will intuitively know what feels right for you and for your retirement.

A Variable Annuity is a contract between you and the insurance company. It's not FDIC insured and the guarantees provided are based on the claims-paying ability of the insurance company. The guarantees I will discuss are twofold. There is a Guaranteed Lifetime Income Withdrawal Benefit (GLWB). The GLWB guarantees that you (and your spouse if you opt for joint life) will have retirement income each month for life. The insurance company sets the level of withdrawal you can take out of the account. This guarantee closely replicates the good side of the Life-pay annuity we addressed previously. The Guaranteed Death Benefit ensures that your beneficiaries will receive what is left in the account when you die. Thus, avoiding the bad side of Life-pay annuities.

Like an Indexed Annuity, a Variable Annuity will have a surrender penalty period. It's typically seven years. If you plan to take a large percentage of your money out of the accounts in the short term, you'll end up paying a surrender penalty during the first seven years. Don't use a Variable Annuity for short term money. Instead, use a Variable Annuity with a Guaranteed Lifetime Withdrawal Benefit for long term retirement income money. Even during the surrender period, you can take out the guaranteed retirement income withdrawal each month. That's what a GLWB is designed for, so there is no surrender penalty on that. It is totally appropriate to use this strategy for retirement income money, whether you need to start taking out your Guaranteed Lifetime monthly income right away or in several years.

The major difference between a Variable Annuity and other annuities we've discussed is, unlike fixed-time or indexed products, a Variable Annuity allows you to fully invest in stock market and bond market investment funds, called sub-accounts or separate accounts. Typically, you will choose to invest in several stock fund sub-accounts and bond fund sub-accounts so you can have the benefit of diversification. These sub-accounts will fluctuate like the investment markets. Some years your sub-accounts will lose money, and some (hopefully the majority of) years they will gain money. This is by design—it is actually a good thing. You'll see why over the next few paragraphs.

Because the account value will go up and down, a Variable Annuity with a GLWB is a long-term retirement income strategy. When the markets and the sub-accounts you have go up, the account value goes up. If the account value moves up, your

GLWB guaranteed monthly amount has the potential to move up as well. If the markets and the sub-accounts you are invested in go down, the account value of the annuity goes down. However, because of the GLWB, the guaranteed monthly income amount stays level. This structure can be a huge psychological benefit for retirees. The consistency of the lifetime income guarantee can provide confidence to stay the course in times of negative markets. Staying the course with the sub-account investments, gives your account balance the best chance to grow throughout retirement.

Retirees do not want the risk of running out of money, which is why these guaranteed lifetime withdrawal benefits have become so popular. They eliminate the risk of outliving your money. They also help eliminate the risk of a few bad years in the market ruining your retirement.

This is a compelling synergistic relationship. The retiree needs a long-term strategy for success in retirement; the security of the GLWB gives the retiree confidence to stay invested in the sub-accounts for the long term.

A Variable Annuity with a GLWB is going to have a higher expense than a pure investment account. If the insurance company provides you with some type of guarantee that makes your retirement more secure, then there will be a cost to do that. In this case the cost is deducted out of your sub-accounts' investment performance. It is not deducted from the monthly income guarantee.

This concept ties back to my team's experience previously mentioned. When we simply explain the Variable Annuity with a GLWB in comparison to a pure investment account to someone, they easily know for themselves which way they lean. The client might say, "That extra cost is not worth it, let's do the pure-investment account." Our response is, "Great, we're totally investment geeks, let's do it." Or they might say, "I love that guarantee and security, plus the chance for growth in the sub-accounts, I'm fine with the cost." Our response is, "That's great too, let's lock in some security of income and still get to decide how conservative or aggressive you want to be in the sub-accounts."

If you decide that you like this idea, remember only a portion of your total investment or retirement money will go into a Variable Annuity with a Guaranteed Lifetime Withdrawal Benefit. You will still want to maintain sufficient funds that are liquid, accessible, Emergency, and Reserve. Your retirement income needs, especially those that are above your social security and pension payments, will help dictate how much additional retirement income you might want to have guaranteed every month.

Now let's look at the role a Variable Annuity with Guaranteed Lifetime Withdrawal Benefits can play in a low-interest-rate, potentially high-inflation rate environment.

We all understand that if you take money out of a low-interest account every year, at some point it will be depleted. Alternatively, an investment account or sub-account can have higher returns. While withdrawing funds for retirement income, higher returns can help offset (or more than offset) those withdrawals. That can help maintain or grow your account value throughout retirement. If the economy slumps or investment markets do poorly, then the account you are withdrawing retirement income from would get hit by a double whammy: negative returns and withdrawals. This would deplete the account value even faster. Retirees do not want the risk of running out of money, which is why these guaranteed lifetime withdrawal benefits have become so popular. They eliminate the risk of outliving your money. They also help eliminate the risk of a few bad years in the market ruining your retirement. Because of that protection, you might feel comfortable using sub-accounts that have the potential for a little more account value growth.

Having the opportunity for more growth in your retirement accounts is a big deal in a low-interest-rate environment. Everything we have talked about up to this point, has been how to squeeze a little more interest rate juice out of an interest rate environment that has been knocked to the ground, smashed flat, and run over by a tractor. The role of this type of product (guarantees combined with investment sub-accounts) in a low-interest-rate environment, is to allow you to go up the risk ladder a little bit with your investment sub-accounts. That will provide the potential for more growth on your account value. It also means that there is more risk of your account value (not the GLWB) having a negative performing year. Going back to my squeezing more return analogy, going up the "risk ladder" with your sub-accounts provides the opportunity to pick the fruit *on* the trees instead of the smashed ones off the ground. To be real, think about it this way: In the current environment, you are not going to get great yields from interest rates that are already on the ground. If you have the safety net under you of a guaranteed income, you may feel more confidence moving up the risk ladder with your sub-accounts to potentially find some higher investment gains that could help you offset inflation and your retirement withdrawals.

Another aspect of a low-interest environment is that the guaranteed amount the insurance company allows you to take each month is going to be a slightly lower percentage amount if you start the contract during a low-interest environment. The guaranteed withdrawal rates during September of 2020, a super low-interest time, were a percent or so lower than if you had started in September of 2019 when interest rates had been slightly increasing for a few years.

The silver lining to that downer is that just like in the Indexed Annuity world, insurance companies are getting more and more determined to make their lifetime income rates attractive. Baby Boomers do not want to worry about running out of money, so insurance companies in this space are driven to make their products attractive. That is a tremendous benefit to those willing to explore the different companies' products to find the best fit. Perhaps most importantly, this is the first strategy we have talked about that can utilize stock-market-type holdings and stock markets have a history of excelling in low-interest-rate environments.

The last point on this is to not make decisions based on what you hear on TV or the radio. These commentators rarely, if ever, sit face to face and walk side by side year in and year out with real people facing real fears. So, they make passionate recommendations from a viewpoint of mathematics and theory. My team and I are experts on the math and the theory, but we work for, plan with, and care about people, not robots. Most of you have lived through the oil embargo in '73 and the Covid crisis in '20 with all the recessions and prosperity in between. Please don't discount those life experiences just because they don't fit into some commentator's theory. I would encourage you to focus on what is in line with your values, goals, and life experiences. Let's finish this chapter with a real-world example.

Real-Life Example #3: Susan's Story

Early in my career, I had Susan come into the office. She'd been divorced for years and her boyfriend, Dan, came with her. One of her accounts was invested in pure stock-market-based investment funds. Susan wanted this money to go to her children when she was gone and felt she was young enough that the account had the chance to grow, "Hopefully about as much as the stock market."

She was certain that she did not want the account in banks, bonds, or lower yielding investments. Susan wanted it to have a chance to grow and was fine with the potential negative periods that growth portfolios inevitably experience. Her biggest worry was that she would pass away when the account value was going through one of these negative time periods. She wanted investments that could grow so that she could pass more assets to her children. She also wanted some kind of death benefit protection for her children if the account happened to be down when she passed away.

We went over numerous ideas: diversified managed portfolios, active allocations, some potential real estate allocations, etc. As we brainstormed, one option we reviewed was a Variable Annuity where the death benefit was a guarantee of the market based sub-accounts or the amount she put in, whichever was higher. Meaning, if she died when sub-accounts were lower than what she started with, the amount she put in would go to the kids. If the sub-accounts were higher than what she initially put in, then the sub-account amount would go to her kids. That was right in line with her goals and addressed her fears. The downside is the death benefit to her kids was not very tax efficient and the annuity death benefit guarantee cost would be a drag of around a percent on her account performance.

Susan really liked it. Utilizing this strategy gave her a lot of peace of mind. Dan, not so much. He had seen on a TV show that you should never have an annuity. He was dogmatic about it. Susan ended up deciding to go with the pure investment allocation. Not a problem for us, and as it turns out, the investment allocation has done great. Account values have gone through some downs and a lot of ups over time. Nonetheless, Susan hasn't even been able to enjoy it. What should have been rewarding has been stressful for her. So even though the numbers look great, in the end, it did not align with her ideals.

I will introduce you to John Lunt, in the last few chapters of this book. One of his great adages is, "The best portfolio is the one that you can live with." You now have permission from me and my team of experts to focus on what you want, what you love, and what brings you peace of mind. Don't let the math, the commentators, or the theory coerce you.

Speaking of "what you love," I love the next section of this book where I get to teach you about different styles, methods, tools, and strategies for investing in a low-interest-rate world. I'm excited—I hope you are too!

Chapter 15

Tool Belts, Tactical Allocations, and Bond Credit Ratings

Early in this book we tackled the question, "Should I pull money out of my investments to pay off a mortgage or should I leave my money invested?" Now we get to address the follow-up question to that. For the funds that you decide to leave invested the question becomes,"Invest in what?" What should you be investing in to secure your future retirement income? In a low-interest-rate, potentially high-inflation-rate atmosphere, I do not think there is a one fix-all solution. Trying a cure-all solution will probably turn into a costly mistake. I'm convinced that the *Secure Solution* in this type of difficult circumstance will require all the tools in the tool box.

My dad worked construction when my siblings and I were growing up. At least, we called it construction. During the recession of the late 70's and early 80's he did anything. Drove anything. Built anything. Cut anything. Hauled anything. I think we called it construction because having a chance to work anywhere was "construct-ive." Many of you remember those days vividly. My memories come from later in the 80's. The economy was starting to improve nationally, a few affluent individuals moving "back home" was a boon for home construction workers in our area, but, on the whole, Southern Utah was still struggling out of the recession. After a stint of no income and living on savings, my dad got a job in town about 15 miles away. We felt blessed that he had found work. The problem was affording gas to drive to town.

So my dad rode a horse to his construction job. I figured he was the last real cowboy; he could ride a horse and build anything.

Starting very young I worked with my dad on our small ranch constructing a lot of things. He got a lot done on the weekends and after he got home from work. I was convinced my dad could build or fix anything—all he needed was a hammer, some bent nails, and a Skil-saw (a type of hand held saw that is powerful, but makes very rough cuts.) I couldn't even lift the Skil-saw and could hardly run a hammer, but in my little boy mind, I could fix anything, just like my dad. I had found a rusted hammer in a dry creek bed, and I had a pair of hand-me-down jeans that had a little loop for the hammer.

When the work in town was finished, my dad's next job was only about five minutes up the road from where we lived. He was part of a construction crew building a beautiful home. I badly wanted to "go help Dad build a house." It was summertime. My mom and I made homemade popsicles with cherry-flavored Kool-Aid. At lunch time, I put my rusty hammer in the loop of my carpenter pants, and we took popsicles up to the construction site to share with the construction crew. After I ate my popsicle, I walked around the construction site collecting the popsicle sticks from the guys so that we could wash them to use for next time.

The workers all showed me what they were doing and the tools they were using. All of those tools! I couldn't believe so many tools existed. One of the workers with wood shavings, and a hint of melted cherry popsicle in his mustache, showed me some of the intricate woodworking he was crafting. I said, "Jeez, I would have done that with a Skil-saw." I was being dead serious, but all his buddies standing around got a good laugh! He laughed too, and then told me, "For a simple job, a Skil-saw will do, but for something complex, you might need more tools."

Well, my friends, creating a successful retirement is "something complex." Anything that requires navigating extended low Fed

Funds rates, growing healthcare costs, the effects of Quantitative Easing, longer life expectancies, long term inflation, and increased market volatility is definitely "something complex." Over the next few chapters, we'll cover concepts that you can add to your retirement toolbox. Specifically, we're going to examine three longer-term investment strategies—tactical allocations, index allocations, and strategic allocations—and how you can best achieve diversification in a modern world.

Let's start with tactical allocation. An allocation is a plan to distribute your money into various investments. A Tactical Allocation moves money from cash to investments and back again following self-established guidelines. There are times a tactical investment allocation strategy can be appealing. For the purpose of this book I'll define a tactical allocation as one that tries to answer the question, "Should I be in or out of the market?" In this case getting "into the market" can refer to buying into either the U.S. stock market, an international stock market, or any of the various bond markets. Getting "out of the market" would mean selling your investments and sitting in cash. You'll often see tactical allocations that are stock-market-based investments because stocks fluctuate up and down so frequently. These fluctuations make it enticing to design a system that designates when you'll be "in" (participating in market gains) and when you'll get "out" (potentially avoiding losses).

Interestingly, another popular market with tactical strategies is the high yield bond market. I have not taught you about high yield bonds yet, so this is a perfect time. High yield bonds have more risk than the Treasuries, mortgage backed bonds, and high-quality short-term bonds that I have discussed previously. Because high yield bonds have more risk, they are one of the favorite asset classes for tactical fund managers. There are a few reasons for this. One is that high yield bonds consistently pay a higher interest rate at issue and typically a higher yield when traded in the open market as compared to more secure, higher quality bonds. Especially in this low rate environment, higher yield is pretty enticing.

If you examine the following chart, you'll note that the credit rating, or the credit risk of a company, is really what makes it either a high quality bond (called Investment Grade) or a lower quality bond (called High Yield). Companies like Fitch and Moody's look at a company's financials and decide how likely they are to either default on their bonds or pay them back. The more likely they are to default, then the lower credit rating that company gets.

	Fitch	Moody's	S&P	DBRS
Investment Grade	AAA	Aaa	AAA	AAA
	AA	Aa	AA	AA
	A	A	A	A
	BBB	Baa	BBB	BBB
High Yield	BB	Ba	BB	BB
	B	B	B	B
	CCC	Caa	CCC	CCC
	CC	Ca	CC	CC
	C	C	C	C

If you have a bond fund allocation built of A-rated and high B-rated companies, you'll have an investment grade allocation to bonds as opposed to a fund of low-B and C-rated companies that can be lumped into a "high yield" bond group.

Now let's look at the difference in yield if you bought investment grade versus high yield bonds.

On the following chart, you find a few yields from August 2020 from the Wall Street Journal as a sample. Notice that the U.S. government credit index—which is a conglomerate of all the government-backed bonds—has an average yield of 1.02%. We kind of expected that, because interest rates are so low and the government's credit ratings are high. It's the disparity in the interest rates that we are interested in. There is a lot of difference in yield that investors can earn by buying bonds that have more credit risk.

Taking the lower risk route by owning bonds of an A-rated U.S. corporation gets you an average of 1.3% per-year yield. A Triple-B-rated corporate bond gets you an average of 2.24%. This is almost double the A-rated yield. Interestingly, A-rated and triple-B-rated, are both considered pretty good, investment-grade credit companies. But that slight difference in credit rating risk makes your yield nearly double.

Now, check out the high yield bond average yield coming in at over 5% per year. Then more than double that, to over 12%, if you jump into the triple-C-rated corporations. These triple-C-rated corporations are usually considered pretty junky. In an interest rate environment when you are happy to get even a 1% increase, you can see why the high yield bonds, including triple-C-rated bonds, are super enticing.

Wall Street Journal Aug 4, 2020	
U.S. Government / Credit	1.02
U.S. Corporate Indexes Bloomberg Barclays Indices	
U.S. Corporate	1.84
Double-A-rated (AA)	1.3
Triple-B-rated (Baa)	2.24
High Yield Bonds ICE Data Services	
High Yield Constrained*	5.438
Triple-C-rated (CCC)	12.679
Bloomberg Barclays data are preliminary. Bloomberg Barclays corporate indexes may be unavailable until midday the following business day.	
*Constrained indexes limit individual issuer concentrations to 2%; the High Yield 100 are the 100 largest bonds	
† In local currency §Euro-zone bonds. ** EMBI Global Index	

Let's address some of the risk of high yield bonds, then we'll see how that fits into a tactical strategy.

One risk associated with high yield bonds is the increased risk that the company defaults on the bond. If you are holding that individual bond you will lose money. In most cases, you are not just going to have one high yield bond that you are holding. It is much more typical to hold a conglomerate of bonds in a fund or Variable Annuity sub-account format. In this case, the risk is less bond specific. In a fund of bonds the risk is more generalized, meaning, it would be statistically more likely to have defaults occur in a bundle of low credit quality bonds than compared to higher, investment-grade or government-backed bonds. It's a broad statement, and there are definitely exceptions, but it's a sound guideline you can utilize. One of the biggest exceptions to this rule was widely publicized in the 2009 subprime mortgage crash. Bundles of bonds sold in 2006 through 2008 were supposed to be high quality, but ended up being mortgage junk. That crisis was a situation of apparently high-quality bonds not being high quality and investors not understanding what they owned.

When it comes to using high yield bonds in a tactical strategy, the fund manager is cognizant of what they own. In typical terms, lower credit quality equals more default risk, and a higher chance that your investment loses money. That's why these investments have a higher interest rate. Who would purchase the extra risk without getting paid for it? Because of their higher risk and higher potential gains, high yield bonds tend to get traded more like a stock than a bond. That means they tend to go through big fluctuations.

Below is a chart of a high yield bond index over a 12-month period from March 2019 to March 2020. The cumulative total return in early 2020 drops significantly from almost 10% positive to negative 13%.

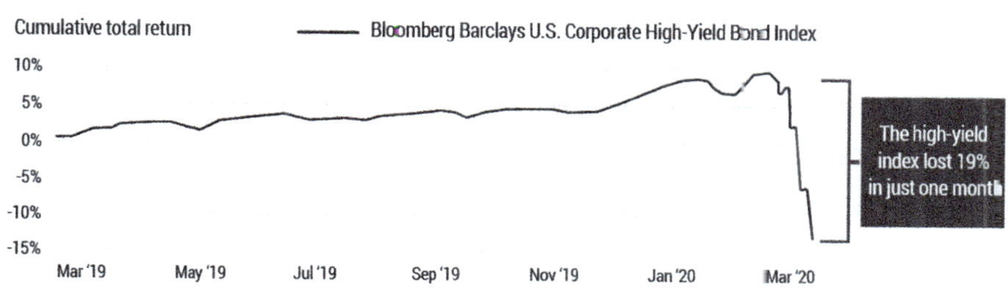

It is pretty apparent that the high yield bond markets have a strong tendency to act more like a stock market index than like a bond market index.

High interest bearing bonds, when you own them, come with the risk that they'll drop in value due to market fears or defaults. That is why high yield tactical portfolios have systems designed to answer the question, "Should I be IN, or should I get OUT?"

It's a compelling strategy. Tactical Strategies were some of the best performers in the 2008 market crash. The economy had been slowing and tactical stock and bond allocations moved more conservative in time to avoid the major crash in Sept 2008. In 2009 they got back in and had huge gains. This potential to mitigate losses and participate in gains can at times make investing in anything other than a tactical fund seem foolish. Do not fall into that trap though. Remember, we are going to avoid one-fix-all elixirs, right? Depending on your situation, a 5% to 25% allocation to a tactical portfolio could be considered reasonable and prudent.

This potential to mitigate losses and participate in gains can at times make investing in anything other than a tactical fund seem foolish. Do not fall into that trap though. Remember, we are going to avoid one-fix-all elixirs, right? Depending on your situation, a 5% to 25% allocation to a tactical portfolio could be considered reasonable and prudent.

Tactical allocations are not a perfect science. Like most things, understanding the laws and patterns in theory doesn't remove the risk associated with the action. Just ask an astronaut if his or her understanding of the laws of physics takes out all the risk, or ask someone who has gone through back surgery, or any other high-risk medical procedure. The science and technology is great, it is amazing, but it doesn't remove the risk. An example of when tactical allocations did really poorly happened in 2015. The S&P 500 stock market index and the Aggregate Bond market index both ended 2015 pretty close to where they had started the year. It was not a flat year, however. There were a lot of big ups and big downs that year, so by the end of the year the markets had about broken even. Not good but not bad. But for tactical allocations it was bad. Almost every tactical allocation got whipsawed in 2015. They would get IN to attempt to catch the uptrend, just in time to participate in the downturn. Then they would get OUT to avoid a long-term downtrend, just in time to miss the up-swing. Many tactical allocations experienced substantial losses during that time period.

In a high interest rate environment, a tactical allocation might not be worth the hassle. You would just buy high-quality bonds and get great returns. When interest rates are low, it is definitely worthwhile to consider if this approach can help you accomplish your goals. Like my carpenter friend taught me, having this tool working for you can certainly help. Just as importantly, be sure to have other tools working for you at the same time.

We are about to explore twelve of those tools over the next nine chapters. Go ahead and grab a popsicle, and settle in, I think you're going to love it.

Chapter 16

Index Allocations

This chapter will be an introduction to investing with indexes. Before I jump into indexes, let me give you the game plan for the rest of the book. You, and my nine-year-old son, are now aware of my disposition to risk "spoiling the plot" so you can know what to expect. Well, here I go again—I think Chapters 26 and 27 are the most important chapters of this book:

Chapter 26 will demonstrate how essential it is for you to reduce your risk during retirement while still maintaining investment growth potential to help offset low interest rates and long-term inflation. Missing that "middle-of-the road approach" is possibly the most costly mistake of retirement.

Chapter 27 will show you how to achieve that middle-of-the-road approach, by utilizing what I think is the most wise, well-researched, and workable way to accomplish it. That chapter will teach you the core strategy for your long-term secure retirement: blending 12 key indexes.

In order to understand those two most important chapters, over the next several chapters I will provide a simple explanation of the 12 major indexes in the investment markets. I will focus on how these individual indexes respond in higher-inflation, low-interest-rate environments. A few of you might use this information as a springboard to further research, understand, and invest individually in those indexes. I will give you some important tips to help you get started on that path. For everyone else—which will be the vast majority of you reading this book—just enjoy gaining a general understanding of these 12 indexes; then, in Chapter 27 we are going to simplify the approach. We're going to hold all 12 indexes equally weighted. The result is going to be so beautiful and inspirational you may shed a tear of joy.

This concludes the Spoiler Alert, thank you for your rapt attention—with that you are practically a member of the Hall family movie night!

Let's set some working definitions for index, tactical, and strategic allocations:

- **Allocation** means a method to distribute (i.e. allocate) your money into different investments.
- A **Tactical Investment Allocation** is answering the question, "should I get in or get out of the markets?" This allocation moves money from cash ("out" of the markets) to investments ("in" the markets) and back again following self-established guidelines. We reviewed the Tactical Allocation concept in Chapter 15.
- A **Strategic Investment Allocation**, that we will cover in Chapters 27 and 28, is answering the question, "which part of the markets should I be in?" These types of allocations decide which investments to invest in, adjust those areas occasionally, but stay invested ("in" the markets) all the time.
- An **Index** is a set of rules and math that, when applied to all the investments in the world, create a *list of investments* that fit those rules. You *cannot* invest in an index.
- An **Index Fund** buys and holds the list of investments, generated by the rules and math of an Index. You *can* invest in an Index Fund.

  (Index Funds can be Index Mutual Funds or Exchange Traded Funds (ETF). Index Funds and ETFs are sold by prospectus. Investors should carefully consider the investment objectives, risks, charges and expenses of

> these funds before investing. This and other important information is contained in the prospectus, which can be obtained from the mutual fund company or your financial advisor and should be read carefully before investing.)

We are going to be spending a few chapters talking about indexes so let's explore them a little more. The index rules are like a filter. An index is a way to create a group of investments that represent some part of the investment universe, by running everything available through the filter. Those investments that fit the rules of the index are the "investments that comprise the index."

This is important because people who often consider themselves to be pretty savvy, have a tendency to say, "I can just buy the index." Then they expect their account to act exactly like the news reports say the index did that day, month, or year. Please don't do that. It actually demonstrates a lack of understanding of what it really takes to "buy" the investments that match up with the rules of "the index."

By its very nature, the rules and math can happen automatically and easily. For example, consider the S&P 500, the Dow Jones Industrial Average, or even the Morgan Stanley Capital International World Index (called the MSCI World index), the math formula for those indexes can happen constantly and automatically.

The mechanics to purchase the stocks at the exact time and exact prices that the index formula calculates, *does not* happen constantly, automatically, nor for free. The reality is, your pricing, when you buy an index fund, will be slightly different than the pure-math index. There will be transaction costs if you go out and purchase every one of the 1,603 stocks that make up the MSCI World Index.

For example, let's pretend the transaction cost is $1 per stock, that's $1,603 dollars just to own the stocks that align with the index. And now, your total investment doesn't quite match the pure math of the MSCI World Index. You're already behind $1,603. If one of those stocks goes down in value enough to fall out of the parameters of the index, guess what, now your current holdings are really not in line with the index. So you sell the one that fell out and buy the new stock that now qualifies to be in. You're doing this at the same time that everybody else tracking the index is selling (pushing the price lower while you're selling) and buying (pushing the price higher when you are buying) the same stocks. This means you won't get the exact pricing used in the math for the current index.

You can see how holding the investments that meet the index criteria IS NOT exactly the same as when you see a news report that references the pure and simple math of the index. To understand the transaction costs associated with owning the investments of an index, let me use a comparison to a real estate investment.

You want to buy a property. You plan to spruce it up and rent it out as a fully furnished vacation rental. Let's say you can buy one in your market for $300,000. You agree with the seller that $300,000 is the price. The simple math would say your return on investment would be the money you make off of the rental minus the $300,000 purchasing price. But I think you'd agree that your total cost to have that investment is going to be higher than just the $300,000. Even if there isn't a real estate agent commission, there is still the cost of making sure you have a clear title, insurance, closing costs, your property taxes, getting the water and sewer and power online, appliances, some furnishings, and who knows what other expenses might pop up. All those expenses reduce the return on your investment, but they are not bad. Making sure you have a clear title and running water are a good thing. They are also an "expense." I would suggest they are a very worthwhile expense. If the expenses did not exist, the investment opportunity would not exist.

It's that same basic concept with an index allocation. In this metaphor, the agreed-to price on the rental property is the equivalent of the mathematical price (like the one that gets reported on the news) of a stock or bond index. You can look at the price of the index in theory. It is helpful. I will often reference the index prices, because they are quick and easy.

However, in our rental example, the expenses that had to be factored in to get a "true cost" were things like title insurance fees, escrow fees, utility charges, and yard maintenance fees. In an index fund the corresponding costs would be things like: stock or bond market exchange fees, clearing houses and trading platforms fees, management charges to reconfigure the holdings when a stock or bond falls out of the index, and the trading cost to rebalance the portfolio in order to keep it aligned with the ever changing pricing of the holdings.

It takes a lot to move that index from math theory to an actual holding in your account.

Index funds do all of that for you! Which is why I think that Index Funds are amazing. The most "expensive" funds are still incredibly affordable for what they do, and now you have access to "no load" index funds. As I've explained, no load, no fee, or load-waived funds still have some cost. I like these funds. I use them. I think they are great. Hopefully, you think they are great, too. They are not free, but they don't have to be. They are still highly affordable, powerful investment *tools* that you can use to address complex retirement investment needs.

I see people make costly mistakes when being hypersensitive to fees. One of the themes of this book is to avoid costly mistakes by deciding what you want and then pursuing it. Let's say the difference in fees on some market-based investment is a tenth of a percent, or even if it's a 1% cost difference, if the fund does what you want, I would say choose the one you like. Be conscious of the underlying cost and the underlying holdings, plan accordingly and choose the funds you feel most comfortable with. There is a lot of media and marketing obsession right now with lowering costs. That is fine, but don't let the tail wag the dog on this. The reality is that even a so-called "expensive" market-based investment, is still amazingly low cost. Just compare the cost of any market-based investment to the cost of starting up another type of investment. Investments like a business, real estate, buying into a franchise, or increasing your education, are great and highly recommended; they all come with a much higher cost than buying into a fund.

Investments like a business, real estate, buying into a franchise, or increasing your education, are great and highly recommended; they all come with a much higher cost than buying into a fund.

Now we know there is a cost, albeit a very reasonable one, for buying into an index fund. You are also aware that fund performance will deviate from the pure-math-index performance. Neither of these issues means that index funds are bad. What is bad, is not knowing these realities when making life-long investment decisions. Let me quickly illustrate two costly mistakes people make with index funds so you can avoid them.

The first example illustrates when investment returns are lower than expected because the investor is using the pure-math returns without realizing the fund returns by definition should be lower.

Real-Life Example #4: The McCarthys

The McCarthys were preparing for their retirement on their own and found an online system that let them answer a few risk-profile questions and enter in their financial planning numbers. The system generated a list of indexes that matched their criteria. They thought if they followed the advice of this program, they'd have enough money for expenses and not run out of funds before they passed on.

They did not realize that index fund investment returns lag the actual index, and that this needs to be accounted for in your retirement income plan.

The McCarthys came to see me after numerous years of retirement, driven mostly by the wife because the husband was not a "stop and ask for directions kinda guy." They said, "We've been using index funds and the internet program said we could do this, but somehow the numbers aren't adding up." These folks were in a tough situation that we had to work through. The culprit of the predicament was simply misunderstanding the nature and the cost of index funds. This was a wake-up call to me. The Baby-Boomer generation has been bombarded by advertisements about how great index funds are, yet they leave out some of this basic information I've shared with you. From that point on, I made it a priority in my educational and speaker engagements to teach these principles to raise awareness that there is an investment performance lag. It's not bad, just know it is there and adjust your retirement income plan accordingly.

The second potentially costly mistake has to do with investment returns that are too high. It will be tempting to find an "index fund" that "outperforms" the index. After all, that sounds exciting. But as enticing as something seems, this type of fund is not following the index. If it is following the index, it's returns will be slightly behind the pure-index returns. Anything else indicates the fund manager is using other strategies in an effort to offset costs plus generate a higher return. Choosing an outperforming type of fund may add risk to your retirement that you do not realize is there.

Those types of funds can be good strategies. Some so-called "expensive" funds have built-in parameters that have demonstrated consistent outperformance over time. They may even have an approach that helps lower the risk of the fund. Index snobs will thumb their noses at an outperforming fund. You and I are just going to see it as another tool in the tool box. There may be an appropriate time for that tool. I'm all for utilizing an outperformer if you recognize what it is and have planned space for a little Red Bull Rampage excitement in your portfolio (I had to throw a shout out to the Red Bull Rampage extreme mountain biking event that happens in my hometown in Utah.). If it is not too much of your investments, this might be advantageous. However, if your intent is to imitate the index in that part of your portfolio, then using an outperformer could turn into a costly mistake. To reiterate, if your goal is to mirror the index, stick to an index fund that, with a little lag, stays aligned with the index. With that, let's jump into a few chapters explaining the characteristics of the 12 indexes that we can combine as a key component of your retirement's "Secure Solution."

Chapter 17

The Agg (Bloomberg-Barclays Aggregate Bond Index)

Let's start with the Bloomberg-Barclays U.S. Aggregate Bond Index, often called the "Agg." Of the three most widely recognized investment market indexes, two are stock indexes (the Dow Jones Industrial Average and the S&P 500) and the other is a bond index (the Agg.) Many retirees have heard the old adage that your "age" is the percentage of your investments that you should have in bonds. So, for a 65-year-old, they would have 65% of their retirement account in bonds or bond funds and 35% in stock funds. If you follow this concept, or if some do-it-yourself retirement software spits out an allocation along these lines, there is a high probability that you will end up with a big chunk of money in a fund that aligns with the Agg Index or something very similar. If that's the case, it's important that you understand how the Agg fairs in the new interest rate world.

Now called the Bloomberg-Barclays U.S. Aggregate Bond Index, in 1986, the Agg started as the Lehman Aggregate Index based on data that went back to 1976 (yes, that's the same Lehman that crumbled in 2008—that's why it's Bloomberg-Barclays now). The concept was to take a measure of all the "investment grade" bonds you could buy in the U.S. The Agg's index rules exclude high yield, foreign denominated, municipal, and certain residential mortgage bonds. It gives you a big picture of the high-grade U.S. bond market. Namely, U.S. Treasury and U.S. agency debt, commercial mortgages, corporate bonds and asset backed bonds. These are generally considered to be pretty good quality investment-grade bonds. Then, you have an index formula that tracks what percent of each of those components make up the total Agg. The important question is, how has the Agg changed in relation to low interest rates and more National Debt?

First off, if you look at historical returns, the Agg has had very few negative years. But let's put that in context. As discussed in Chapter 10, if interest rates go down, the value of bonds go up. So if interest rates are trending down, then your bonds' values will be getting pushed higher and higher. Consequently, when I tell you the Agg has had very few negative years, it's important to think about what interest rates have been doing since the Agg came into existence in the '80s. Interest rates have come way down. I'm certain any of you that bought a house during that time can vividly remember what rates were in the late '70s and '80s as compared to now. The historical returns of an Agg bond fund have been inflated (sometimes greatly inflated) by an interest rate environment that kept dropping lower and lower and lower.

With the Fed Funds rate at 0% to 0.25%, there is no room left for your bonds to get a tail wind from lower interest rates. I think this is one pitfall of using the "your age in bonds" rule. If you had 65% or 70% of your allocation in the Agg for the last 30 years as interest rates went down, that worked out pretty well. To have that amount allocated to the Agg now, with interest rates flat and then moving up could be a big issue.

There are still two more components to factor into your decision making.

The next thing to consider is duration. When interest rates finally do move a little, they can't (hopefully) go anywhere but up. Also, from Chapter 10, recall that the longer your bonds are (duration), the *more* they go *down* if interest rates go *up*. If you have a lot of long duration bonds and interest rates move up, that could be ugly for your portfolio.

Next is yield. If your bonds are still getting a good yield, then the interest you are receiving might be worth the risk of longer duration.

Let's look at some numbers to understand why the Agg is positioned in a "worst of both worlds" scenario. On the following chart, we have the effective duration of the Agg compared to the effective yield over a 15-year span. The average duration of the Agg is a solid line. The Agg's duration was around 4.5 years back in 2004. As you can see on the chart, the Agg's duration has been climbing. More duration is more risk when interest rates finally move up in the future. That is, unless you are getting more yield to compensate you for the risk. Take a look at the Agg yield. It is the dotted line, and it has moved much lower. Back in 2004 and 2005, you were making 4.5% or 5.5% and you had less duration risk. Since then, the yield has been pushed lower through Quantitative Easing. As of mid 2020 the average yield to maturity on the Agg is under 1.5%. That is a 70% reduction in yield.

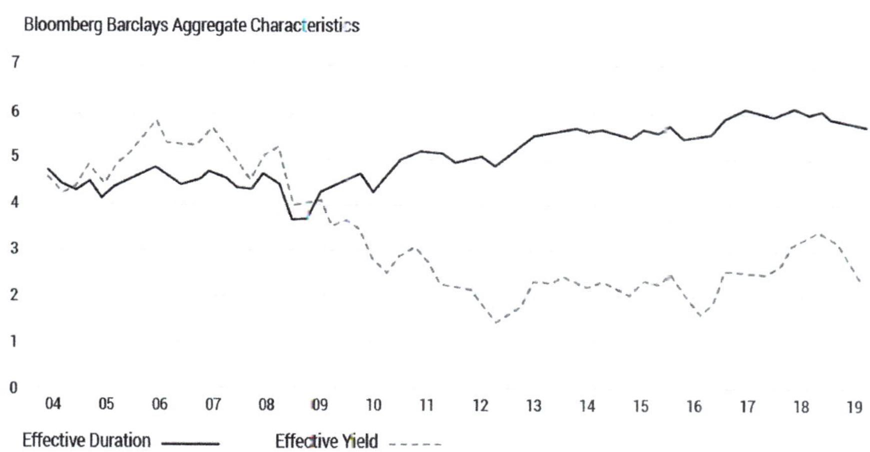

The interest rate risk, the longer duration risk, and the low yield make buying into the Agg *now* a much riskier investment than it has been over the last 30 years.

The interest rate risk, the longer duration risk, and the low yield make buying into the Agg *now* a much riskier investment than it has been over the last 30 years.

The last thing to be cognizant of, is how much the government and government agency debt portion of the Agg has ballooned. The Agg Index is intended to be a representation of all the investment-grade bonds out there, based on their respective percentage of the market. As we discussed in Chapter 4, National Debt is nearly a $30 trillion-ton elephant. In order for the Agg to be reflective of that, there is a big percentage of the index in government and government agency debt. For example, in March of 2021, one Agg-based index fund called iShares Core U.S. Aggregate Bond Index Fund had almost 40% in U.S. Treasuries, *plus* another 20% in Federal and Government Mortgage Agencies. The end result is that current Agg-based index funds have less diversification, higher interest rate risk, and lower yields than in years past.

Now that you have this knowledge of the Agg, let's address a few potential courses of action. Decide if you want to stick with the Agg. That could be fine for quite some time. If you decide to do that, then pay attention to the FOMC meetings. At some point, they might hint at increasing rates. That would be the point you may want to re-allocate away from the Agg and other long duration bonds. Along these lines, check your 401k bond holdings. A lot of 401k and other retirement plan asset allocations have the Agg as the go-to bond holdings. The Agg has been the mainstay of bond holdings for 30 years, so it has become one of the main, and sometimes the only, bond option inside 401k platforms. If you have been making your 401k more and more "conservative," you might inadvertently be adding more and more interest rate risk and duration risk.

Another reasonable action is to move away from the Agg now. One way to do that would be to replace it with a short-duration alternative. We talked about those in Chapter 10. You won't get as much yield on a shorter duration holding, but you're not getting much yield from the Agg either. Short-duration bonds can help lower your duration and interest rate risk. In connection with using a shorter-duration bond fund, another way to move away from the Agg is to utilize the allocation concept that we'll cover in Chapter 27. This allocation only has a 1/12th allocation to traditional U.S. bonds. The other bond allocations do not have the same risk profile as the Agg.

Let's talk about those other bond indexes starting with Treasury Inflation-Protected Securities.

Chapter 18

TIPS (Treasury Inflation-Protected Securities Index)

Time to learn about Treasury Inflation-Protected Securities (TIPS). My team and I went out on a limb early in 2020 by teaching in our presentations, video content, and educational courses that low interest rates are here to stay for a while. Then on August 27, 2020, Fed chair Powell's announcement confirmed our planning strategies. In the past, if inflation nudged up to 2%, the FOMC was quick to raise interest rates, even if that meant curtailing business' abilities to borrow, expand, and, most importantly, hire more people. The new position by the Fed is to allow the labor market to continue to expand, and hold tight on the current low Fed Funds rate, even if inflation runs above 2%.

As a result of this announcement, it's fair to say you have to plan for two challenges during an extended period of low interest rates. First is the increased reality that the costs of things you buy are going to keep creeping even higher over time. Second, the interest rate you get on traditional savings is not going to be high enough to keep pace with inflation. This FOMC announcement could be good for the labor market, stock markets, and for businesses that want to borrow and expand, but it has the potential to make navigating retirement even more perilous. A bit discouraging, I know, but the good news is that, starting with TIPS, the remaining 11 market indexes you will learn about have the potential to benefit from, or at least tolerate well, a low-interest-rate, higher-inflation rate period.

Let's look into the Barclays U.S. TIPS Index. There are multiple funds that track the TIPS Index. TIPS are considered very high credit, and very secure because they are Treasuries backed by the Federal government.

So, how do TIPS work? A TIPS is a bond that has an interest rate, *and* the value of the bond itself goes up with inflation. The Federal Government calculates a Consumer Price Index (CPI). The CPI is a gauge for inflation because it is tracking how much things cost for consumers. As the CPI goes up, the value of your TIPS increases by the same amount. Plus, the TIPS have an ongoing interest rate that is based on your bond value. This is an important point. As the bond value goes up with inflation, the more interest you will get. Even though the interest rate stays the same, it is now on a higher inflation-based value. That means more money in your account to help offset increasing costs.

TIPS do have some interest rate risk. In this extremely low-rate environment, their yields can be low and even negative at times. Over the long haul though, assets like TIPS should perform better than conventional Treasury bonds in a rising interest rate environment, because their inflation adjustments provide better price protection.

In the following chart, you'll note the average CPI has been on an overall continuous upturn since the 1960s. It is easy to see the dotted line on this chart relentlessly climbing upward. Even more relevant than seeing a chart illustrate inflation, we see it happening in real time all around us. Many of you have watched inflation playout dramatically in your life. My clients tell me they could have never believed how much houses, cars, gasoline, and food would increase in price during their lifetimes. One client told me, "If I had dozed with Rip Van Winkle and awakened at a car lot, I'm certain I would have thought it was a nightmare, not a reality."

Another interesting way to make this point is to look at the solid jagged line. It measures the percentage change in inflation each year. Along the far right side of the graph is the "Change in Consumer Price Index" numbers that correlate to the solid jagged line. There are two times on that chart (in the 1920's and another in the 1930's) when the change in average inflation was negative (below zero). Every other percentage change, whether it's 15%, a 5% or a 1%, is a reminder that inflation has been relentless.

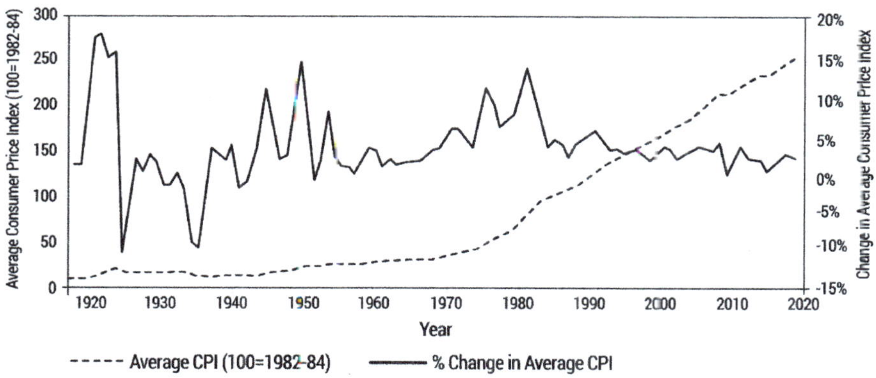

Source: Bureau of Labor Statistics

There really needs to be a consideration for this trend in your retirement investment strategy.

It is super important to note that, historically, the Fed has been very quick to increase rates if inflation gets close to 2%, so you wouldn't lose money on your low yield investment for too long. Look at the more recent years on the previous chart. The solid line has been fluctuating between near 0% and 3%. That is likely going to change. The Fed's policy revision to let inflation run higher without immediately raising rates means you need to

---

It is super important to note that, historically, the Fed has been very quick to increase rates if inflation gets close to 2%, so you wouldn't lose money on your low yield investment for too long.

---

have a strategy to help address this inflation risk. That's where a TIPS index fund could come into play. It can be particularly helpful in the context of the multi-index fund portfolio that we are leading up to.

Chapter 19

International Bonds Index

With international, or non-U.S. bonds, there's a lot to choose from. In this type of environment, non-U.S. bonds can be a nice compliment to your other U.S. bond and TIPS holdings. For this chapter, I am just lumping the spaghetti bowl of all non-U.S bonds on your plate, even though every noodle is technically pretty unique.

As a quick example, I will mention two indexes that are both "non-U.S. bonds" but are quite a bit different. First you have the Emerging Markets Bond Index (or EMBI). It's a benchmark index for measuring the total return performance of international government and corporate bonds that are issued by specific emerging market countries.

Second is the S&P/Citigroup International Treasury Bond Index Ex-U.S., an index designed to measure the performance of Treasury bonds issued in local currencies by financially developed countries outside the U.S. This is important because these bonds are non-U.S. Treasuries but they're in developed countries, not emerging markets like EMBI, and they are issued in local currencies instead of in U.S. dollars.

We could fill another ten books on international bonds, but what you really need to understand is that there is likely a place for non-U.S. bonds in your investments during this extended low-interest-rate and possibly inflationary era. I'll give you some very basic concepts concerning international bonds. Just know they're not all encompassing. Here are three concepts I'd like you to understand about international bonds.

First, is that you can often find a higher yield by going to non-U.S. Treasuries and non-U.S. Corporation bonds. For example, the EMBI can certainly yield 5% or better. There is more risk (hence more yield) in a non-U.S. Treasury than a bond backed by the U.S. government, so it is not an apples to apples comparison. To continue the fruit analogy, maybe a nice compliment to U.S. apples would be some foreign oranges, giving you a little more juice without going too far on the risk spectrum. Meaning, done right (with an eye toward understanding and mitigating risk) there are some opportunities to increase your yield in non-U.S. bonds.

Second, the FOMC's indication that they will keep rates low could be very beneficial for foreign and especially emerging market countries, because it means they can also issue debt at lower rates to fund their economic growth. Put simply, if you and I could get a high rate on U.S. bonds, then we would not even look anywhere else. Another country would need to issue debt at rates that are much higher just to get our attention. However, because the U.S. rates are low, non-U.S. bonds can be attractive to investors at rates that are slightly higher than U.S. rates, yet still very beneficial for the issuing countries' economies.

You have to add one more item to the equation: currency.
Currency risk versus currency potential benefits.
A country's inflation is generally correlated
to its currency becoming less valuable.

The third concept is something that often gets forgotten. You have to add one more item to the equation: currency. Currency risk versus currency potential benefits. A country's inflation is generally correlated to its currency becoming less valuable. If the U.S. goes through a period of moderate inflation, it could have a devaluing effect. If the U.S. dollar devalues, then it buys less, especially on imported goods. So there is a devaluing effect for those who live here, but also in comparison to other countries. You've probably noticed this when you travel and encounter different exchange rates between countries.

You can invest in currency-hedged or currency un-hedged foreign bonds. The reason you typically lean towards currency-hedged as a U.S. investor is because, if the currency of the country from which you purchased the bonds drops in value relative to the U.S. dollar, any return from the bonds will be reduced by the same degree as the currency devaluation. The previous FOMC policy of curbing inflation has also kept the U.S. dollar stronger relative to other countries.

In this anticipated inflationary scenario, where the U.S. dollar weakens somewhat compared to the country from which you purchased the bonds, using un-hedged funds could further increase your bond funds value. This increase can be beneficial for your retirement success. Hence the reason we're incorporating non-U.S. bonds to the list of indexes to consider in your retirement allocation.

There are a lot of moving parts to making smart financial decisions. It can, and often does, get overwhelming and discouraging. So let me share a funny story to lighten your heart and hopefully encourage you.

I grew up on a small ranch. My family did not ski. My wife's family did, does, and always will ski. My wife's father was the mountain manager for a ski resort in Northern Utah. He passed away when she was in high school. Some time later, the mountain manager at a ski resort in Southern Utah became my wife's step-dad. So, needless to say, a few years into our marriage, I learned to ski as an adult. In fact, my oldest daughter who was four or five at the time had actually learned to ski the year before I did. While I was learning how to ski, my daughter and her cousins were cruising on the bunny slopes with me. Those of you who have skied know that the quickest, easiest way to control your speed and direction when you are learning is to put your skis into a triangle with the ski tips practically touching. It's called a "snowplow," or more often a "pizza." My daughter had mastered the "pizza slice" and she and her friends were zipping all over the place. I, on the other hand, was an adult man, who had achieved a high level of athletic success in life, yet was becoming increasingly frustrated.

It was only the bunny-slope. It wasn't a long ski-run. It wasn't even steep. My wife didn't really need to turn, and could just control her speed with a simple snowplow. I weighed enough, and I was rookie enough, that I had to make a lot of turns to stay moving slowly. I wore out *quick*! My wife is an excellent ski coach. She instructed me, encouraged me, and reassured me that refining turns and speed control on a gentle slope would serve me best for skiing steeps for decades to come. So I kept at it. At the end of one torturous run, my daughter asked, "Mom, can I ride the ski lift up with Dad?"

My wife said, "Yes, but don't let him wipe you out while he's trying to get on the lift." With that inspirational poke, we got in the lift line. Thankfully my daughter and I got on the lift with no incident.

As soon as we were both seated, my daughter put her tiny, pink-mittened hand on my leg, and said, "Dad, we need to talk. My friends and I are really tired of waiting for you." She paused and gave me an adorable smile. "So if you'll just put your ski's like this," she put her mittens up with the thumbs apart and the fingertips touching to demonstrate a snowplow, "and just go straight down the mountain like us, you'll do better. No more of this turning back and forth, and back and forth all the way down the mountain." As we got ready to get off the lift at the top of the slope, she patted my leg and said, "Follow us, and Dad, just try to keep up."

I loved it. What a great memory of being shown up by my five-year-old daughter. As parents, we're so proud of them, we wouldn't want it any other way. Just so you know, I did NOT keep up and I did NOT catch up. But I did NOT give up and now the whole family skis together on a regular basis.

By reading this book, you are likely right in the middle of one of those adult learning experiences that can (if you're anything like me) be frustrating. I would suggest that the most important take-away from this fun story is giving yourself permission to *not* master every detail on your "first run down the mountain." We have all had experiences where guidance and repetition through a slow and steady process is actually better and faster in the long run. In fact, when you have someone else, or even the voice in your head, telling you to go faster, sooner, or riskier, remember this story and give yourself permission to stick to the bunny slopes a while longer before attempting the steeper stuff. Stick with the basics. Get a coach. Just don't give up. I have no doubt that you are having more success keeping up with all this education than I was trying to keep up with my daughter and her cousins!

Let's continue with a few more chapters laying the foundation of how different indexes respond to a low-interest-rate, higher-inflation-rate environment. Then we'll put it all together in Chapter 27.

Chapter 20

Natural Resources and Commodities Indexes

It is time to talk about a couple indexes that are probably not on your radar and are very likely not in your 401k or IRA investments, but maybe they should be. I'm talking about Natural Resources and Commodities. Let's start with the ultra-simplified basics. The general use of Commodity and Natural Resources funds is to help hedge against inflation.

I think I just heard you say, "Hallelujah, Telton, since the FOMC's revision in August of 2020 I've been worried about pockets of hyperinflation and an overall extended period of moderately increased inflation!" I knew that's what you were thinking, we must be bonded.

When we start to put all the tools together in Chapter 27, we will look at a chart with 20-year investment performance data on all 12 indexes. You may notice that the Natural Resources Index (6.4% average return) has had more attractive returns than the Commodities Index (3.6% average return) over the last 20 years. If you had to choose one index, you would likely go with Natural Resources. You don't have to be limited to just one though. If you want to hold one fund that tracks a broad-based Commodities index and one that tracks a Natural Resources index, today's index funds make it very doable and cost effective to hold both types.

Another reason to potentially use only a Natural Resources fund is that there is often Overlap between the two indexes. When two funds that are tracking different indexes end up having the same or very similar holdings it is called overlap.

Here's an example of overlap in the Energy Sector of a Commodities index and a Natural Resources index. Starting with the broad market Bloomberg Commodity Index, the target weights heading into 2021 are as follows: **Energy 29.9%,** Hard and Soft Grains 29.88%, Industrial Metals 15.56%, Precious Metals 19%, Livestock 5.58%. (Information available at *https://www.bloomberg.com/company/press/bloomberg-commodity-index- 2021-target-weights-announced/*)

If we compare that to the S&P Global Natural Resources Index, you'll see the overlap. The following pie chart shows the breakdown of the S&P Global Natural Resources Index toward the end of 2020: 63% Materials, **30.1% Energy**, 5% Consumer Staples, and 2% Real Estate.

Sector* Breakdown

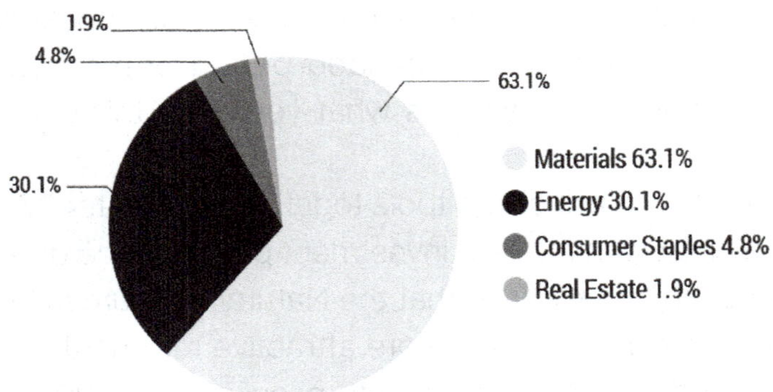

*Based on GICS® sectors
The weightings for each sector of the index are rounded to the nearest tenth of a percent; therefore, the aggregate weights for the index may not equal 100%

The Natural Resources index has 30.1% in the energy sector. The Commodities has a 29.99% allocation to the energy sector. If you are investing in both index funds you would have a heavier weighting in Energy, than if only using one index fund or the other.

There are two approaches to addressing overlap. One route is to just hold a Natural Resources Index Fund and you'll get some of the benefits of both types of indexes. The other approach is that the overlap of holding both index funds could be appropriate because Commodities and Natural Resources combat inflation in slightly different ways.

Commodities prices have historically *reacted* to supply shortages, which often causes price increases to happen in bursts. We have certainly experienced that recently in response to COVID shutdowns that disrupted the supply chain and dramatically increased prices on certain commodities.

Natural Resources indexes incorporate companies that deal in Consumer Staples. These companies are *proactive* in building demand for their products. This tends to create more consistent profits over longer periods of time.

Both approaches are going to have seasons of success during the next 30 years. The management style we use for clients will make adjustments from one index to the other in response to changing seasons. You may elect to just hold both fund types throughout retirement.

For Commodities and Natural Resources, the blessing and the curse of today's index market is that there are a number of very focused Commodities and Natural Resources fund strategies. Unknowingly investing in a focused fund when you think you are getting a broad-based fund could be a costly mistake I would like to help you avoid. Let's compare broad-based funds (that I have described so far) with focused funds.

A focused fund is great for specific situations, while a broad-based fund has the potential for gains to help offset overall inflation over a long time—like a 30-year retirement.

As an example of a focused fund, you can have a "commodity index fund" that solely tracks the price of silver bullion, or the price of a gold bar. Silver and gold are commodities so they fall into the Commodities Fund category.

In a focused fund that tracks the price of physical silver, 100% of the price of that fund will be based on silver. If you compare that to the broad-based Bloomberg Commodities Index that we reviewed earlier in the chapter, the broad-based Bloomberg Commodities Index has holdings in agriculture, energy, industrial metals, livestock, *and* precious metals. The percentage target weights from earlier in the chapter had Precious Metals as 19% of the broad-based index.

Historically speaking, 19% is the largest weighting Precious Metals has ever had in this broad-based index. Yet, even at this high precious metal weighting, silver is only one part of the total allocation to precious metals. Due to that, there is actually only a 4.35% allocation to silver in this broad-based index. That is drastically different from a 100% allocation to silver in a silver-focused fund.

If silver takes off like it did leading up to the third quarter of 2020, the focused fund has a substantial positive return, while the broad-based index was negative due to the energy, livestock, and agriculture holdings. This actually makes sense. Funds focused on precious metals will typically do well during times of economic uncertainty. Meanwhile, the broad-based fund should be a help against inflation long term. The time period leading up to the third quarter 2020, although great for speculating on the price movements of silver, was not an inflationary period.

I want to leave this chapter with one aspect that connects the inflation we are seeing now and the low interest rates: the cost to store Commodities and Natural Resources. During an extended period of low interest rates, the cost to finance storage of a stockpile of commodities is low, which then pushes prices on the commodities up. Think about it first in terms of the opposite situation. If it costs me a bunch of money every day (higher interest rate environment) to store a bushel of cotton, then I will lower the price to sell it more quickly. That way it's not costing me to store it every day.

If the cost is low to finance the storage of my cotton stockpile (i.e. a low-interest-rate environment) then I will stockpile it until there is demand built up. Then I'll sell into the demand to get higher prices, thus pushing the price of Commodities and Natural Resources higher.

Higher prices mean you will be able to buy less with your dollar—unless, of course, you're pulling your dollar from an investment account that has moved up with the cost of Commodities and Natural Resources. That's where you can succeed where others won't. I'm convinced that your success in retirement is dependent on knowledge of the situation and some simple strategies to help implement that knowledge. It may not always mean making the most money, but it does mean making your money work for you.

Speaking of making your money work for you, let's take a minute to understand traded Real Estate. You may not be surprised by my enthusiasm at this point, but just so you know: I love this next chapter.

Chapter 21

Exchange-Traded Real Estate

One of my favorite allocations to an investment portfolio, when it is appropriately implemented in a retirement income plan, is real estate. I have no problem with local real estate, rentals, commercial properties, raw land, things like that. Those types of investments have their pros and cons like any investment. Yet, so many retirees come to me and say, "I'm done with my rentals. I'm so sick of managing my property—or worse, managing my manager who is supposed to be managing my property." Financially, real estate has been good to them but they want something truly passive. There are several options for people in this situation, but one investment I believe worth exploring is Exchange-Traded Real Estate.

Exchange-Traded Real Estate index funds are totally liquid, accessible, and available, any given day that the stock and bond markets are open. If the markets are open, you can buy it or sell it. There's no rental contract, you don't have to sell it and then close through a title company, or even have a real estate agent agreement. This kind of real estate trades just like a mutual fund or an exchange-traded fund, it's liquid and totally passive. Those are two major perks.

Because it is easily sold or bought any day, you can see the value of this real estate fluctuate daily. Some might see that as a downside, especially during times when the price is going down. Yet, in reality, local real estate values fluctuate all the time as well. The difference is that you can't see the price ticking up or down on your computer screen throughout the day.

Because it is easily sold or bought any day, you can see the value of this real estate fluctuate daily. Some might see that as a downside, especially during times when the price is going down. Yet, in reality, local real estate values fluctuate all the time as well. The difference is that you can't see the price ticking up or down on your computer screen throughout the day. Even if you are checking Zillow every hour to see if your home price has changed, it's not quite the same. Zillow and appraisals use what other homes around you have sold for as a means to determine a price. With an Exchange-Traded Real Estate index fund the basis behind the price you see is somebody on the other side of the screen actually offering to buy it, at that price, right now.

I personally have both Exchange-Traded Real Estate and I own local real estate. I like them both. But I don't like it when the benefits of local real estate get misrepresented. I could never in good conscience, or as a licensed fiduciary, get away with saying the half-baked examples of great returns that real estate folks are so cavalier about tossing around. Let me share an example from a conversation I had with a real estate friend of mine a few years back.

Real-Life Example #5: James

James was telling me he hated anything that traded on the market (like Exchange-Traded Real Estate.) He had worked with a different financial advisor, wasn't happy, and now was talking to me. The other advisor had helped him get a mutual fund for around $3,000 a couple years prior and it lost money so he cashed it out for around $2,900. In his mind, it had been a big waste of money to use exchange-traded investments. James said he only liked to have "something real," something physical where he could "go kick the tires." I told him, I totally get that, and could work with him to maximize his retirement income plan in other areas.

Then he tells me, "Listen, I bought a piece of real estate for $35,000 and now I'm getting offers for $350,000."

There's nothing I can do like that, I thought to myself. *Wow, that sounds pretty impressive!* I was curious and sincerely wanted to understand the details. So I asked, "You've never lost money on it?"

"No," he said.

"Wow, and how long did you hold it?" I asked, because it sounded like he was "flipping" it after a couple years.

James responded, "I bought it in 1979."

"And every year it kept going up in value?" I asked.

"Oh, yeah," he assured me.

"What about during the early 80s recession?" I wondered.

"Are you kidding?" he said. "Nobody would have paid anything for it then. Nobody had any money."

"Okay, so it did go down in value some at that time," I clarified.

James goes, "Well, I wasn't going to sell it at a loss. So, no, I didn't lose money on it."

"Got it," I said, holding back a smile at this point. "And you bought it for $35,000 and never had to put any other money into it other than paying the property taxes each year?"

"Well, I had to get a property zone change and then I built a duplex on it."

"Oh, how much did that cost?" I asked.

"Around $120,000." To me it sounded like that was probably a while ago, so he has hopefully been getting rent for all those years since then.

At this point, I better understood what was going on. The value of his property had truly gone up and down, but all he could see was that a $35,000 property turned into a $350,000 gold mine.

In reality, it's an asset that did fluctuate in value, especially during recessions, and actually cost $35,000 plus $120,000 to build on, which equals $155,000. Hopefully he got some cash flow each year that rents were higher than expenses and vacancies. As for asset appreciation, I would put it like this: a $155,000 investment turned into $350,000, over about 38 or 39 years. That is around a 2% per year rate of return.

Let's compare James' investment to a liquid Exchange-Traded Real Estate index (exchange-traded Real Estate is also called publicly traded, because it is readily available for the public to purchase or sell in the open market). Exchange-Traded Real Estate typically comes in the form of a real estate investment trust (REIT) fund. REIT is usually pronounced "reet." Let's look at a generic real estate investment trust index provided by the National Association of Real Estate Investment Trusts (NAREIT). This chart covers the same time frame as James' real estate investment. It's not a perfect comparison, but it gives you a good idea. If $100 (on this chart) turns into $7,000 by 2018, then the $155,000 that James put into real estate would have turned into $10.8 million. Not $350,000. $10 million!

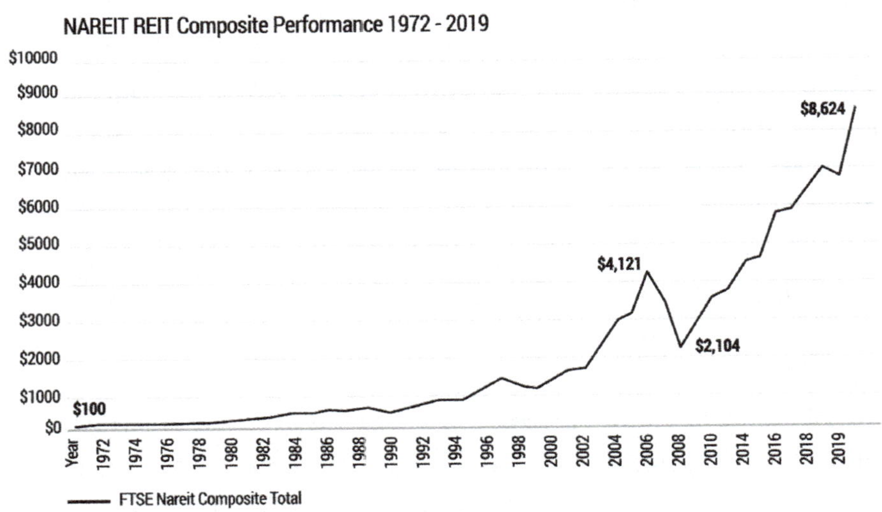

That is a really strong return for an investment that did not require any time, property taxes, zone changes, construction, or maintenance. This is the pure index, not a fund, so any fund that tracked this index would have lagged a little because of implementation costs. I can live with that! We certainly don't know what the next 30 years will bring, but we do know that this REIT index experienced years with negative returns in the past. James would have had to maintain the same "I'm not gonna sell at a loss" type of mentality to experience the full benefit of this index. Perhaps even more compelling, is that James could have sold in 2008, a horrible time, and he still would have received $3.2 million from his original $155,000. That's a bit more than the $350,000 or so James could have sold his property for a couple years back.

So, let me reiterate, I like local real estate. I invest some in it, but it's important to be real about its pros and cons. Let's also not underestimate the potential benefits of utilizing a REIT index.

Another thing to know is that, in general, REIT index funds will usually pay some type of a dividend because the underlying properties will have, as a general rule, some kind of rent that is then passed through to the owners of the fund.

REITs will be either domestic (U.S.) properties, non-U.S. properties, or both (called a global REIT).

REITs, like Commodities and Natural Resources funds, can be focused or broad based. Categories include commercial, specialized, multi family, industrial, retail, and healthcare properties. A broad-based approach would include most or all of these categories. A focused strategy would have just one.

Let's look closer at Dow Jones Global Real Estate because it will give us the biggest picture. The following pie chart shows the property-type breakdown.

Sector* Breakdown

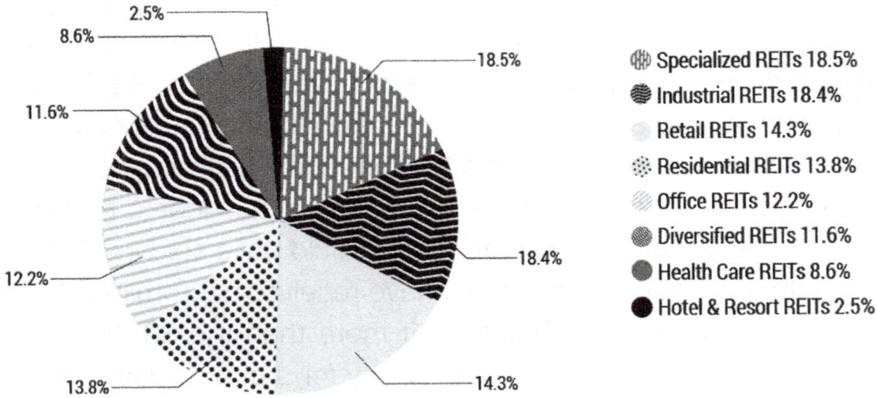

*Based on GICS® sub-industry
The weightings for each sub-industry of the index are rounded to the nearest tenth of a percent; therefore, the aggtegate weights for the index may not equal 100%

You'll note the chart is made up of Specialized, Industrial, Retail, Residential, Office, Diversified, Health Care, and Hotel and Resort REITs. There's quite a variety represented in this index, and there are a variety of funds that focus on the individual sectors. Or you can use a fund that tracks the whole index for broader diversification throughout retirement.

The next aspect of diversification to consider is: diversification by country. You may want to focus on just one segment of the globe or just one country. Alternatively, a global index, as you'll note in the following table, takes a very broad approach with 20 different countries. However, notice the way this Dow Jones Global Real Estate index is configured, the U.S. is still, by far, the largest player.

Country Breakdown

COUNTRY	NUMBER OF CONSTITUENTS	TOTAL MARKET CAP [USD MILLION]	INDEX WEIGHT [%]
United States	149	839,297.15	65.3
Japan	62	129,379.46	10.0
Australia	28	87,096.65	6.4
United Kingdom	32	62,929.25	4.9
Singapore	36	71,705.55	3.8
Canada	29	43,695.31	1.7
France	7	33,035.32	1.7
Hong Kong SAR, China	6	24,055.59	1.6
Belgium	7	18,452.17	1.3
South Africa	14	7,467.69	0.6
Mexico	5	8,143.34	0.5
New Zealand	5	6,365.77	0.4
Spain	3	8,533.03	0.4
Thailand	5	6,194.77	0.3
Germany	2	3,280.20	0.3
Malaysia	6	8,183.17	0.2
Netherlands	4	2,129.62	0.2
Saudi Arabia	6	2,351.35	0.1
Ireland	2	1,662.19	0.1
South Korea	3	1,394.15	0.1
Israel	1	655.16	0.1
Turkey	3	1,303.35	0.1
Italy	1	383.65	0
China	1	339.07	0

Based on indexed constituents' country of domicile

A global REIT index fund is a pretty compelling, publicly traded, totally liquid, broadly diversified opportunity to easily own some of the best real estate around the globe. This type of index fund is worth understanding and potentially including in your retirement strategy.

Low interest rates make purchasing the underlying real estate more affordable. If rents stay the same, because of long term leases, but the financing cost is lower because of low interest rates, then, all things being equal, REITs have the potential to pay higher dividends (basically, the equivalent of rent). As a bonus, the underlying real estate in general, has a strong tendency over long periods of time to at least keep pace with, or greatly outpace, inflation. Keep this asset in mind. Your retirement may end up thanking you.

Chapter 22

U.S. Stock Indexes: Large, Mid, and Small Capitalization

Large Cap, Mid Cap, and Small Cap—these are not baseball hat sizes. I'm talking about the different U.S. stock market indexes. Stock market indexes can be categorized based on the financial size of the companies in the index. The word "cap" refers to "capitalization". To determine if an individual stock is a Large, Mid or Small Cap, take the stock's share price and multiply it by the number of shares available. That gives you, typically, a pretty big number. If that number is over 10 billion, it is called a Large Cap company. There is technically a "Mega Cap" designation that's $200 billion or more, but those companies will show up in the Large Cap indexes. For example, Microsoft, Amazon, and Apple are in the trillions, and Facebook, Walmart, JPMorgan, and Johnson & Johnson are in the hundreds of billions of market capitalization, but they all will show up in your Large Cap index.

If the cap amount is in the $2 to 10 billion range, the company is a Mid Cap. A Small Cap is when the capitalization ranges from $250 million to $2 billion. As you can see, Small Cap companies are still fairly large and shouldn't be confused with a speculative penny stock or a start up.

Indexes are made with rules that take these caps into account. For example, the S&P 500 index is based on specific parameters, like:

- Take the 500 largest cap publicly traded companies in the United States.

- Allocate each company proportional to their size so the larger they are, the more weight they have in the index.
- Examine the index annually to see if there is a need to reconstitute any of the companies held.
- Adjust the allocations of all 500 on a quarterly basis to try to align with the updated cap weights of all 500 companies (in-case some companies have grown more than others).

If you want to invest in the 500 companies that make up the S&P 500, you'll invest in an index fund that tries to mirror the index's constituents. A couple examples would be State Street Global Advisors S&P 500 Trust Exchange Traded Fund (SPY) or Vanguard S&P 500 Exchange Traded Fund (VOO). I mention these two funds simply because they are well known in the investment world. Amazingly, these are just two of hundreds, if not thousands, of funds that invest in the Large Cap stock space. Easy access to thousands of great funds makes this a wonderful time to be pursuing your retirement goals. At the same time that we are facing complex challenges, we also have a robust set of tools to accomplish the task. With today's investment technology, you can literally create an index for any segment of the markets you want to track, then create a fund that mirrors the index.

> People and pundits have a tendency to refer to "the market." Usually, they are talking about the S&P 500 as a barometer for all U.S. stocks. This is fine for convenience, but I would also suggest that you recognize the inaccuracies of calling the S&P 500 "the market."

Let me make one observation about well-known indexes. People and pundits have a tendency to refer to "the market." Usually, they are talking about the S&P 500 as a barometer for all

U.S. stocks. This is fine for convenience, but I would also suggest that you recognize the inaccuracies of calling the S&P 500 "the market." First off, if we want to refer to U.S. stocks as "the market" then the S&P 500 is only incorporating Large Cap stocks. It is totally missing the Mid Cap and Small Cap indexes, which are pretty important indexes as you'll see in the rest of this chapter. An Index that could be a more accurate representation of the U.S. stock market is the Wilshire 5000 Total Market index. This index is important because it has so many holdings. This makes it much more reflective of the U.S. stock market's performance. Schwab Funds, iShares by Black Rock Funds, and Vanguard all have exchange traded funds that track the Wilshire 5000.

The second reason that referring to the S&P 500 as "the market" is a bit misleading is because there are at least 12 major markets. The 12 indexes we are reviewing are representative of that. Recognizing and utilizing the benefits of all 12 major market indexes will be particularly important for creating secure retirement income in a low-interest-rate world. After you have implemented the 12 index strategy explained in Chapter 27, the next time someone is talking about what "the market" is doing, you can make a mental note that the conversation is probably only addressing Large Cap U.S. stock. Large Cap U.S. stock is great and wonderful. We love it and utilize it, but it will likely only be 1/12th of your broadly diversified retirement allocation.

It's time to address another potential candidate for 1/12th of your retirement portfolio: U.S. Mid Caps. Some of the best stocks in a Large Cap fund today were once Mid Caps. Before that, they were Small Caps. The great news is that, even if you missed owning a company as it grew from a Small Cap to a Mid Cap, you can still have great investment success by holding that company as part of a Mid Cap index fund. In your Mid Cap fund, your portfolio gets the chance to move up in value with these companies as they try to grow into Large Caps. Some well known Mid Cap indexes are the Russell Midcap Index (RMCC) which covers 800 companies with market capitalization between $2 billion and $10 billion, and the S&P Mid Cap 400 Index (MID).

Small Cap index funds could likely have a place in your long-term plan as well. Small Cap index funds are considered pretty aggressive growth indexes. There are a lot of specialized Small Cap indexes that focus on certain components of the Small Cap market. As an example, a popular growth play is to focus on innovative tech companies that might boom from the transition to 5G networks or self-driving cars.

Probably the most recognized broad-based Small Cap index is The Russell 2000 index. Rules to arrive at the 2000 holdings of the Russell 2000 are as follows. First off you eliminate the very small companies (Micro Caps and penny stocks). This leaves you with about 3,000 of the biggest companies. Then, to get rid of the Large Caps and most of the Mid Caps, you eliminate the biggest 1,000 of those companies. Now you're left with the Russell 2000 index. It's considered a pretty solid broad market exposure to the Small Cap world of U.S. investing.

Chapter 23

U.S. Stock in a Low-Interest-Rate Environment

Now that we've tackled three major indexes of the U.S. stock markets (Large, Mid, and Small Caps), let's look at how they act in a low-interest-rate, high-inflation environment, starting with combating inflation. As with everything else we've covered in this book, these indexes are not immune to the changing interest and inflation environments. The key is figuring out if you can make those changes in the economy work for you during your retirement years. It is safe to say that at the very least, you need to be aware of the potentially beneficial role that stock index funds could play over an extended period of time during your retirement.

On the following chart, you'll find the compound annual returns from 1926-2018 with a timeline along the bottom that includes some major national and world events. This chart portrays the general idea that stocks have been very good over long periods of outpacing inflation enough to have true asset growth, with some room for taking retirement withdrawals.

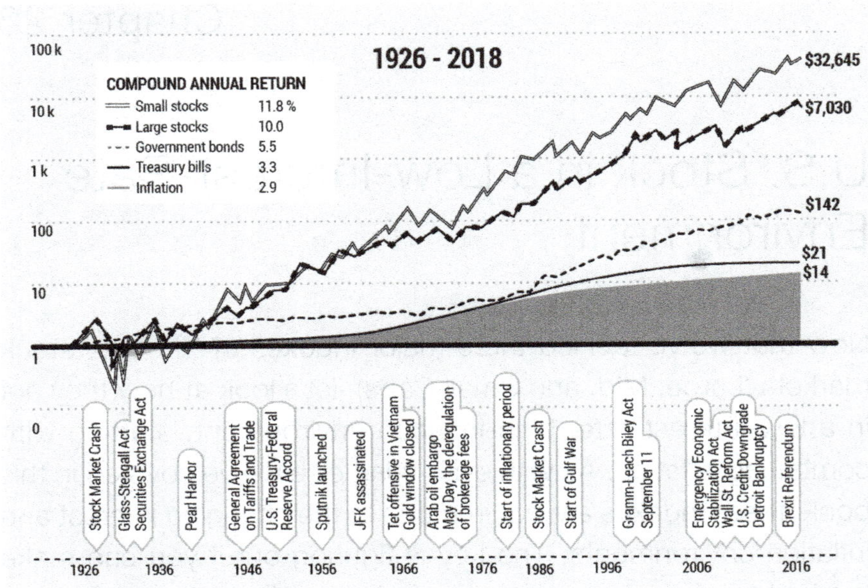

One way to understand why Large, Mid, and Small Cap U.S. indexes could perform well in this low-interest-rate environment, is that stock prices increase when companies are profitable. Although their short term values fluctuate greatly depending upon the emotions of the masses, over a 15 or 30 year retirement, stock values keep moving higher as companies find ways to increase profitability.

Profitability is the ability to sell a product for more than the cost to produce it. Companies use debt to accomplish this, so the less expensive debt is, meaning the lower the interest rates are, the easier it is to finance company production at a profit. When you own stocks or a stock index you are an owner who participates in the increased profit and increased company growth that is available because of the low-interest-rate environment.

When it comes to inflation, too much inflation too fast can be bad, while moderate inflation can be good for stock indexes. Too much inflation (hyper-inflation) is bad for everyone. It is bad for the consumer because everything costs more and their income hasn't caught up yet. It is bad for companies because it takes a while to adjust prices to still be profitable. Then, once a company does adjust prices, consumers may not want to buy their product at higher prices. This type of fast moving, high inflation is what the FOMC is monitoring and managing. Although this type of hyper-inflation is a potential concern, former FOMC chair and current Secretary of the Treasury, Janet Yellen, when talking about avoiding a lengthy period of hyper-inflation said, "I think the Fed is going to win out on that." I think I agree with her. The FOMC certainly has the authority, tools, lessons learned from history, and the disposition to curtail hyper-inflation.

The research suggests that when measuring the inflation adjusted stock index returns, the decades with the best returns occurred in time periods where inflation was a little above 2%.

A potentially positive scenario for stocks is indicated by the FOMC's policy adjustment in August 2020 to allow for some moderate inflation. It allows for inflation to run a little beyond 2% for a time, because it has been less than that for several years. For investment geeks, that is compelling and here's why: The research suggests that when measuring the inflation adjusted stock index returns, the decades with the best returns occurred in time periods where inflation was a little above 2%. On its own, inflation can be pretty bad on a fixed income in retirement. That's why utilizing stock index allocations, in connection with your risk tolerance and your long-term income goals, could be critical to maintaining your long term retirement income.

I know it's hard to believe, and I know sometimes it seems crazy to be optimistic. Even my sense of reasonable, research-based optimism occasionally gets taken into the back alley and mugged by the fear mongering of the media. I get it. However, please know, these fundamental economic principles you have just learned are compelling reasons that we could be in for some good times ahead. You are certainly well on your way to having a knowledge base to recognize some ways to benefit from this environment.

One more way to potentially benefit from a higher inflation rate is utilizing a value stock index. There is a body of research, mostly done by Eugene Fama and Ken French, which suggests Value stocks have a trend to perform better during higher inflationary periods than Growth stocks. One way to research the opportunity in stock markets is to look for companies that are priced below their competition and below their broader market. These are called Value stocks. By contrast, stocks with high earnings, even if their stock prices are really high, are called Growth stocks. The research suggests that in a low inflation time period, Growth indexes outperform. Value stocks have a strong tendency to perform better during higher inflationary periods. The good news is that blending Large, Mid, and Small Cap indexes will provide a nice allocation to both value and growth stocks. Another piece of good news is that in Chapter 29 I will give you what I think is a simple but sweet idea for tapping into the potential benefits of value stocks during different seasons.

For now, the key takeaway is to remember that from a historical framework Large, Mid, and Small U.S. stocks have great potential for growth as we move through this low-interest-rate, moderately-higher-inflation-rate environment.

Chapter 24

Non-U.S. Stock Indexes

Now that I've covered the major bond, natural resources, real estate, and U.S. stock indexes, let's finish by going over the opportunities in non-U.S. (sometimes called foreign, or International-exU.S.) stock. Non-U.S. stock is typically divided into two indexes: Developed Markets and Emerging Markets. Developed Markets are countries that have large economies, high income per-capita, and investment markets that are easily accessible and efficient. The U.S. is a developed market. Non-U.S. Developed Markets would include Australia, Germany, the UK, and Japan. Emerging Market countries have smaller economies than Developed Market countries, but are large enough to have investment markets. These investment markets are not quite as liquid and efficient as Developed Markets. Mexico and South Korea are examples of Emerging Markets. In addition, the acronym "BRICS" (Brazil, Russia, India, China, and South Africa) references the five major Emerging Markets. There's likely a place for both types of non-U.S. stock indexes in your long-term retirement portfolio.

Let's start with understanding how these asset classes can react to interest rates, inflation and strength or weakness of the U.S. dollar.

Like most stock indexes, foreign companies will generally benefit from a low-interest-rate environment. If companies can borrow and expand by utilizing low-interest-rate financing, then there is the potential for more profits and more gains, which get passed on to the stock index fund holders. As consumers re-engage after the COVID crisis, an extended low-interest-rate environment will likely be good for non-U.S. stock indexes.

Holding foreign stock indexes can also be profitable for U.S. investors during seasons when the U.S. dollar is weaker. Increasing National Debt and higher inflation rates make the U.S. dollar weaker compared to other countries' currencies. A slightly weaker dollar does not help when you are vacationing outside the U.S., and it is not great for the U.S.'s collective purchasing and bargaining power in the world economy. It does, however, help your foreign stock indexes be more profitable for you. With the FOMC's disposition to keep interest rates low, (even if it means inflation runs a little higher and the dollar gets a little weaker) having an allocation to foreign stock indexes becomes even more important.

A slightly weaker dollar does not help when you are vacationing outside the U.S., and it is not great for the U.S.'s collective purchasing and bargaining power in the world economy. It does, however, help your foreign stock indexes be more profitable for you.

One more feather in the cap of foreign indexes is that non-U.S. indexes have performed well when the FOMC finally does start to incrementally raise the Fed Funds rate. A situation where the FOMC raises rates quickly or the dollar strengthens rapidly would hurt the performance of your non-U.S. investment indexes. Much more realistic is that the FOMC will incrementally and conscientiously increase interest rates without rapidly increasing the U.S. dollar's value. That type of environment has seemed to correlate with strong investment performance in the non-U.S. stock markets.

As a reference for this concept let's look at an example from Emerging Markets. The next chart shows the FOMC's Fed Funds rate (Fed Funds Target rate) as the solid line. The Fed Funds Rate percentage is on the right side of the chart. The years are along the bottom. The grey areas are times when the FOMC is raising rates (Rate Tightening). Find 2005 on the bottom of the chart. The FOMC started raising rates at that time. You can see the solid line start at just under 2%, and then stair-step up to around 5% by 2008. The dotted line is the Morgan Stanley Capital International Emerging Markets Index (MSCI EM Index). The emerging markets index experiences a lot of growth during the time period of rising rates. The value of the MSCI EM index is on the far left of the chart. From 2005 to 2008 the MSCI EM index grew from basically 20,000 to 50,000. Although not quite as dramatic, the other grey periods showing Fed Funds rate increases, also demonstrated positive performance in the emerging markets index.

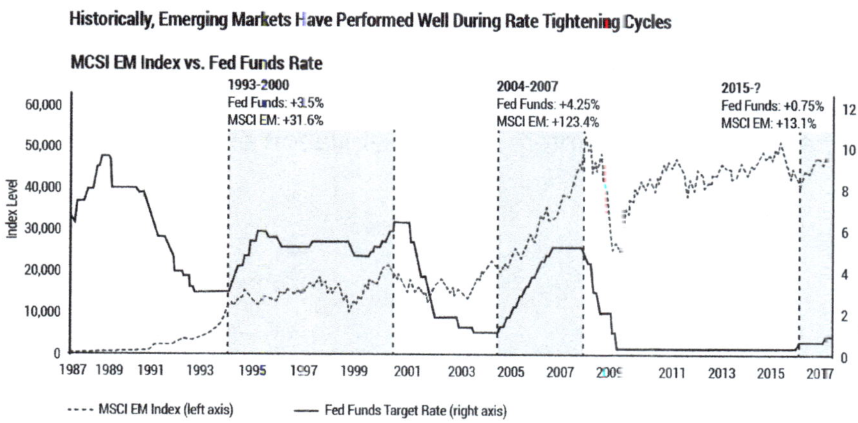

That is compelling information. There is a hope and a concern that at some point, interest rates will begin to slowly increase. We would like some parts of the portfolio to benefit from that. Non-U.S. stock indexes could be the ticket to do just that.

You are now familiar with the 12 major market indexes:

- Cash equivalents, like savings accounts and money markets
- U.S. bonds, like The Agg
- Inflation Protected Bonds

- Non-U.S. bonds
- Natural Resources
- Commodities
- Exchange-Traded Real Estate
- U.S. Large Cap stocks
- U.S. Mid Cap stocks
- U.S. Small Cap stocks
- Developed Non-U.S. stocks
- Emerging Market stocks

Over the next few chapters, you'll learn crucial concepts on the *why* and *how* of buying, holding, blending, and fine tuning index funds into Strategic Allocations. All of this is in order to maximize your potential to get through a lot of happy retirement years, even in the midst of a low-interest, higher-inflation environment.

Chapter 25

Transforming Indexes into Strategic Allocations

I am super excited to show you a couple ways to accomplish a strategic allocation. I think these types of allocations will be indispensable to your long-term retirement success. Strategic allocations help us answer the question, "what part of the markets should you be in?" I'll walk you through a couple strategies that my team and I have found to be very effective.

Exchange traded markets are so available, public, and so near instantaneous, that bids to buy "discounted" stock, or groups of stocks, would increase stocks' value so quickly that it would no longer be at a discount.

Let's start with Phase 1 strategic allocations (in Chapter 28 we'll get to Phase 2). The first way to approach Strategic investing is on the basis that there are no "deals" in the exchange traded markets. "Exchange traded markets are efficient," is the core concept. In this approach there are no stocks on sale. No Black Friday deals, no Labor Day liquidations, or President's Day promotions. Because if discounts did exist, everybody would buy them in a hot second! Exchange traded markets are so available, public, and so near instantaneous, that bids to buy "discounted" stock, or groups of stocks, would increase stocks' value so quickly that it would no longer be at a discount. This phenomenon is called the "efficient market hypothesis" and it is the reason that indexes exist.

In an index investing approach, we don't know which stocks will go up and which will go down so we just buy all of them in that segment. If we want all the Largest Cap U.S. stocks, we use the S&P 500 Index fund; all the Small Cap U.S. stocks, buy a Russel 2000 fund, etc. Efficient markets hypothesis is basically what created the Index Fund investment approach that we use today.

Index funds give us an "aggregate of all the stocks" profit potential, but what about the volatility risk of a single index? Many clients come to me wondering this. They understand that holding 500 stocks in a fund helps reduce their risk of a large loss by "not having all your eggs in one basket." They also remember when the Dow Jones Industrial Average and S&P 500 dropped dramatically in the '80s on Black Monday, in the 2000's, again in 2008, and in the early part of 2020.

You might say, as the reasonable human that you are, "I don't care if this index had five hundred holdings or five trillion holdings, I don't want to live through that." That's a valid feeling. I would agree, you need some ways to further reduce risk and still have a chance to grow your accounts up to and throughout retirement.

That is why we start mixing, matching, and blending different indexes, at different times, and during different seasons. The basic concept all started with some really cool math, and a Nobel Prize won by Harry Markowitz who came up with modern portfolio theory. In my own words, it states that we can lower risk by holding more assets than just one type, and at the same time, maintain a more than equal percentage of the return or growth potential. This theory generally blends stocks and bonds to lower risk.

I want to show you a way to benefit from a theory that I think is even cooler than Markowitz's approach (To say "better than Markowitz" is nearly heresy in the investment portfolio world, but that's a chance I'm willing to take for your retirement success.) I'm going to rely heavily on the brilliant research of Dr. Craig L. Israelsen. His research examined the effects of combining not just a stock and bond index, but instead giving all 12 major market indexes (the ones I've been teaching you about) an equal allocation. The data reveals that giving all 12 indexes an equal voice over long periods of time, like your retirement, has created a very successful ensemble. Though Dr. Israelsen hasn't won the Nobel Prize (yet) I think he certainly deserves a "you're a genius" Stanley Cup-size trophy.

Let's go over this chart from Dr. Israelsen's research. It looks at seven of the 12 indexes that we have discussed so far. These seven indexes are the Core Asset Groups and they have the longest histories. They go back 50 years, so this chart consolidates 50 years' worth of data.

Starting on the far-left column is "Large U.S. Equity." The number directly underneath "Large U.S. Equity" is 10.60. The average annual return of Large Cap stocks over the last 50 years is 10.60% per year.

In the far-right column "Equally Weighted Multi-Asset Portfolio," you can see that 9.65% per year is the annual average return over the last 50 years when blending the seven core indexes.

Year	Large US Equity	Small US Equity	Non-US Equity	US Bonds	Cash	Real Estate (REITs)	Commodities	Equally Weighted Multi-Asset Portfolio
50-Year Average Annualized Return (%)								
	10.60	10.88	8.68	7.40	4.74	11.63	6.73	9.65
50-Year Standard Deviation of Annual Returns								
	17.04	21.26	21.59	6.48	3.51	18.45	24.69	10.20
Worst 1-Year Return (%)								
	-37.00	-33.79	-43.38	-2.92	**0.03**	-39.20	-46.49	-27.60
Worst 3-Year Cumulative Return (%)								
	-37.61	-42.24	-43.32	**4.39**	**0.14**	-35.61	-55.60	-13.37

Past performance is no guarantee of future performance.

Source: Craig Israelsen 7Twelve™

Remember that the return percentages on the chart are just the math from the index. There is an additional cost to turn math into index funds held in your portfolio. To compare apples to apples we'll just use the straight index math from the chart: 10.6% per year over 50 years in Large Caps and 9.65% per year for the Multi-Asset Portfolio.

The next line down is not an interest rate or a profit, it is the "50-Year Standard Deviation of Annual Returns." To keep things basic, the higher the standard deviation number, the more risk an allocation has.

The 50-Year Standard Deviation for Large U.S. stock (far-left column) is 17.04.

The Standard Deviation of an Equally Weighted Multi-Asset portfolio (far-right column) is 10.2.

Just by blending indexes (as is done in the multi-asset portfolio), the standard deviation (the risk) decreased from 17.04 to 10.2. This means the multi-asset blend only had 59% of the risk compared to the Large U.S. stock asset. Pretty impressive! We love reducing risk! It gets even better, though. Mathematically, if you took 59% of the risk, you should only get 59% of the return. But the multi-asset strategy averages 9.65 % per year compared to the Large U.S. stocks 10.6% per year return. When you blend the right indexes, you are within 1% of the Large Cap U.S. stock return. You are getting the benefit of 91% of return with only 59% of the risk. That's a huge deal. That's the benefit of Phase 1 strategic investing!

Chapter 26

Why Mitigating Market Volatility and Maintaining Growth Potential Matters

I have focused quite a bit on strategies for increasing returns to help offset potentially higher inflation while we're in a low-interest-rate environment. Reasonable returns are important. In addition, I want to demonstrate why reducing risk without going too conservative is so important. Most retirees have heard that they need to get more and more conservative as they get closer to retirement. That is pretty well known, but frankly, that concept is often emphasized too much. In many cases, moving more and more money to bonds and cash could be damaging because a lot of 30-year analysis is based on interest rates being high then decreasing during

In many cases, moving more and more money to bonds and cash could be damaging because a lot of 30-year analysis is based on interest rates being high then decreasing during retirement. Well, as I hope you've gathered by now, higher interest rates decreasing over time are the polar opposite of the environment you're going to be retiring into.

retirement. Well, as I hope you've gathered by now, higher interest rates decreasing over time are the polar opposite of the environment you're going to be retiring into. Overdoing the concept that you need to put more and more assets into cash and bonds as you near retirement, though it certainly can help reduce *some* risk, might end up being a costly mistake to your long-term retirement goals.

Let's compare three retirement Account Scenarios.

They are the same in these ways:

- All three retirement accounts start with a $500,000 account value.
- All three retirees need the account for retirement income.
- All three retirees start withdrawing $25,000 each year from the account for retirement income.
- To help offset inflation a little bit, all three retirees increase their withdrawal amount by 3% each year.

Now for the differences:

- Account A, on Chart 1, utilizes an investment portfolio that fluctuates. It goes through some nice growth in early years, then experiences years with large losses later on.
- Account B, on Chart 2, utilizes the same hypothetical investment returns as Account A, but *in reverse*. This is to demonstrate the effect of experiencing large losses early on in retirement.
- Account C, on Chart 3, is representative of taking retirement withdrawals from an account that is very secure. It has *no negative years*, it does not experience investment losses, but in a low-interest-rate environment it gains very little interest—2% each year.

Check out Chart 1. The solid line is the account value. This account demonstrates the benefits of having growth potential in your retirement accounts. You are able to take $25,000 a year from this account, increase that amount each year, and 26 years into retirement you have maintained, and even grown, your retirement account value. The positive impact and even the downright necessity to have some type of growth potential in your retirement account cannot be understated.

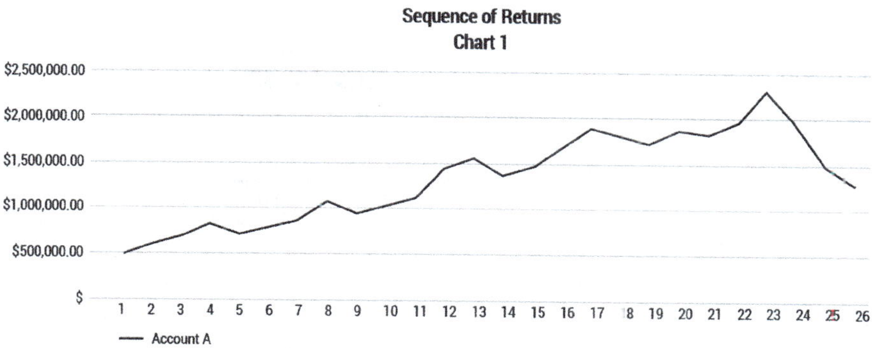

The chart is hypothetical. The average annual return is equal to 8.0% with a standard deviation of 14.25% and does not reflect the performance of an actual product or account, or the taxes and other fees that, if applied, would reduce performance. The chart also reflects a hypothetical withdrawal of 5% at the beginning of the year. Starting in year 2, the withdrawal is increased by 3% to illustrate a hypothetical rate of inflation.

Next is Chart 2. In this chart, Account A is now a dotted line for reference. Account B is the same exact withdrawals, the same increases for inflation, and it would have been the same overall average return as Account B, but large investment losses early on in retirement *combined* with retirement withdrawals depletes the account. The negative-compounding effect of losses and withdrawals drives this account to zero way sooner than life expectancy. Reducing risk and volatility (the Standard Deviation we talked about last chapter) would have been critical to success in this retirement scenario. Now you can see why we are so passionate about finding ways to reduce volatility.

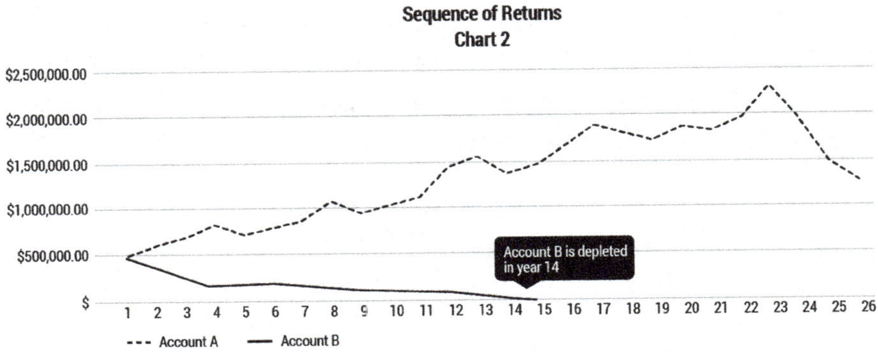

This chart is hypothetical. Performance for Account B illustrates an inverse of the sequence of hypothetical annual returns of Account A. Without distributions, the average annual return is equal to 8.0% with a standard deviation of 14.25% in both scenarios. The chart also reflects a hypothetical withdrawal of 5% at the beginning of the year. Starting in year 2, the withdrawal is increased by 3% to illustrate a hypothetical rate of inflation.

Last up is Chart 3. Here is the kicker: If you saw Account B and said, "I'm going to avoid volatility at all costs. I'm just going to go to bonds and cash." I can understand your thinking, but that won't actually solve your problem.

It might have worked when interest rates were high, but they are low and will very likely stay low. A mixture of cash (at .15%) and secure bonds (at 2% to maybe 4%) might pay around 2% per year. In Chart 3, Account A and B are still included for reference. Account C is the solid line. This account represents a "no risk" scenario with no volatility, basically no Standard Deviation, and a 2% per year interest rate.

When taking retirement income withdrawals from the account, Account C is actually depleted even faster than Account B!

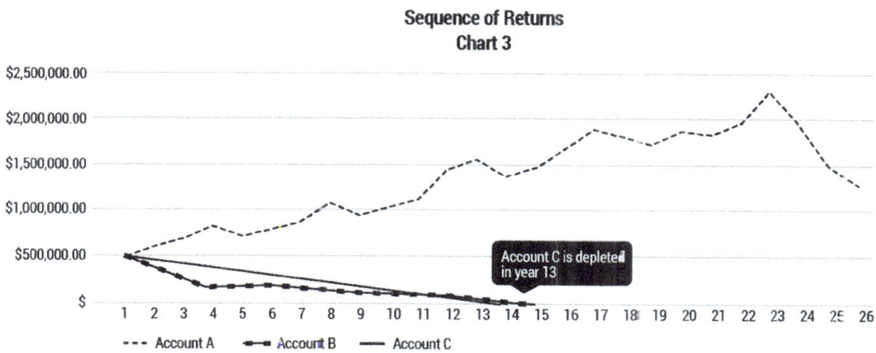

This chart is hypothetical. Performance for Account C illustrates an account that goes through no negative years. The chart also reflects a hypothetical withdrawal of 5% at the beginning of the year. Starting in year 2, the withdrawal is increased by 3% to illustrate a hypothetical rate of inflation. This chart also illustrates the account having a fixed growth rate of 2% applied to the account after the withdrawal.

Reducing volatility *and* maintaining reasonable growth through a strategic allocation is a BIG deal. Utilizing a pure-index stock approach can provide great potential returns, but experiencing losses at the wrong time could be damaging. Reducing the risk of your accounts could be quite important to your retirement goals, but over-allocating to bonds or cash might end up actually being detrimental.

The good news is that creating a strategic allocation that blends seven core indexes has, historically, given us attractive and reasonable returns, and lowered volatility. This type of approach gives us a middle-of-the-road path between Account A and Accounts B and C.

In the next chapter, I'll expand the seven-index strategy to a 12-index strategy from Dr. Israelsen and show you how successful a middle-of-the-road approach can be.

Chapter 27

The 7Twelve Portfolio

You made it to Chapter 27! I'm super excited to share it with you. A couple chapters ago, I previously introduced Dr. Craig Israelsen's research on seven major asset classes that had practically 50 years' worth of historical data to dissect. The end result was that, with purposeful and strategic diversification, this seven-index allocation over long periods of time had returns almost as good as the S&P 500 (growth potential), and more importantly, it achieved those returns with substantially less standard deviation (lower volatility or risk).

Using seven indexes reduced the risk significantly. But think about the impact that could be made when we add five more indexes to these seven core indexes. This will further broaden diversification while maintaining growth potential. We'll turn back to Dr. Israelsen's research for this. He calls it the 7Twelve portfolio.

I have made the case that this is the most important concept of this book. When you think about all of the information you've learned—about navigating loans, how to maximize your short term liquid accounts, how to utilize a Guaranteed Lifetime Withdrawal Benefit—it's all really good information. Any of these concepts, when applied to your situation, could have a substantial positive impact on your retirement success. So when I say that the 7Twelve allocation might be the best part of the book, that's a pretty big statement.

The next chart displays the 12 major market indexes that make up the 7Twelve.

On the next chart, note the 7 Core Asset Groups: U.S. Stock, Non-U.S. Stock, Real Estate, Resources, U.S. Bonds, Non-U.S. Bonds and Cash. These are the original seven indexes that we explored two chapters ago. Those 7 asset classes have the longest historical data. Then, notice that four of those 7 asset groups are large enough that they need to be represented by more than one index. That was not the case 50 years ago. But as our investment markets have developed, the seven core assets were not fully representative of the major investment opportunities. For example, the U.S. Stock Asset class has three major market indexes: Large Cap, Mid Cap, and Small Cap. In order to fully utilize the investment opportunities that exist in each asset class, we will end up with 12 major indexes. Each shaded box on the chart represents a major market index. To turn the 7Twelve into an investment portfolio, you buy an index fund that aligns with each of the 12 indexes.

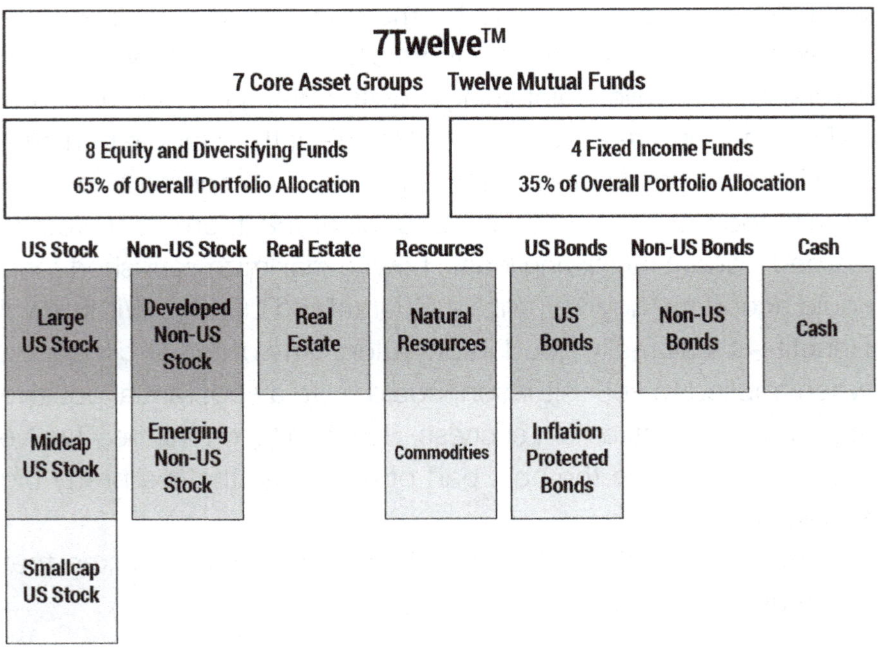

The name 7Twelve® is a registered trademark belonging to Craig L. Israelsen

I've spent quite a bit of time going through the 12 indexes one by one, but the magic happens when you blend them. And to retire comfortably in a low-interest-rate, high-inflation-rate environment, you need a little magic in your life.

Let's look at another chart from Dr. Israelsen. This chart has data for all 12 indexes, and each index is represented by an index fund. Some of the 5 new categories we added have shorter historical data. Due to that, this chart shows data from 2000–2019

The chart shows the Standard Deviation (the measurement we are using to gauge risk) for all 12 indexes. Plus the emphasized bar on the chart shows the Standard Deviation of the 7Twelve Portfolio. Blending all twelve allocations in the 7Twelve creates a risk profile that is much lower than any of the growth asset classes. The Large U.S. stock standard deviation is 17.78 compared to the 7Twelve at 11.99, that is 32% less risk than the Large U.S. stock and way less than Real Estate (at 18.74) or Emerging Stock (at 30.35). The only thing demonstrating less risk over this time period are the bond allocations, and because of the low-interest-rate environment that we are in, you just can't realistically put all your money in low-yielding bond assets and retire securely. So from a risk perspective, this approach is very encouraging.

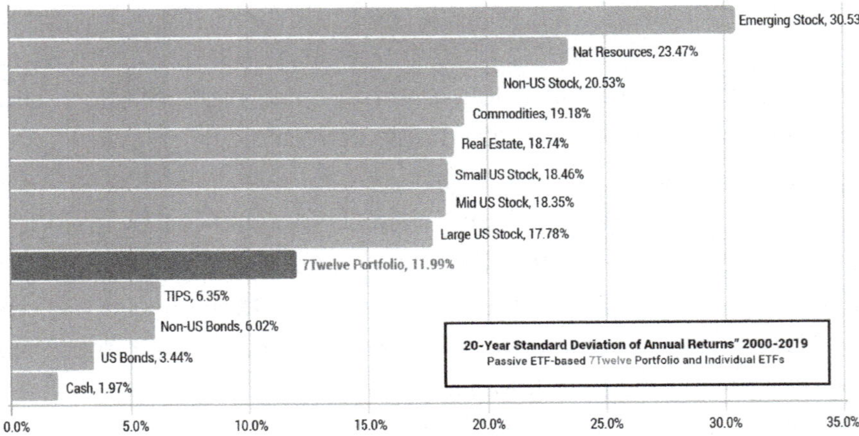

The name 7Twelve® is a registered trademark belonging to Craig L. Israelsen
Past performance of investment products or indexes does not guarantee future performance.

The multi-asset blend has a better return and lower risk historically!
For your secure retirement prospects, this is beautiful.
This is an appropriate time to shed a tear of joy.

Equally encouraging is that from an investment growth perspective, the 7Twelve strategic allocation is near the top. This next graph shows the investment performance of all 12 index funds. The highlighted bar is the investment performance of the 7Twelve. The investment performance for the 7Twelve portfolio is even above asset classes like Large Cap U.S. stocks. Large U.S. Stock, in the last chart had higher risk than the 7Twelve (so you'd think it would have a higher return). Not so. This is great news: The multi-asset blend has a better return and lower risk historically! For your secure retirement prospects, this is beautiful. This is an appropriate time to shed a tear of joy.

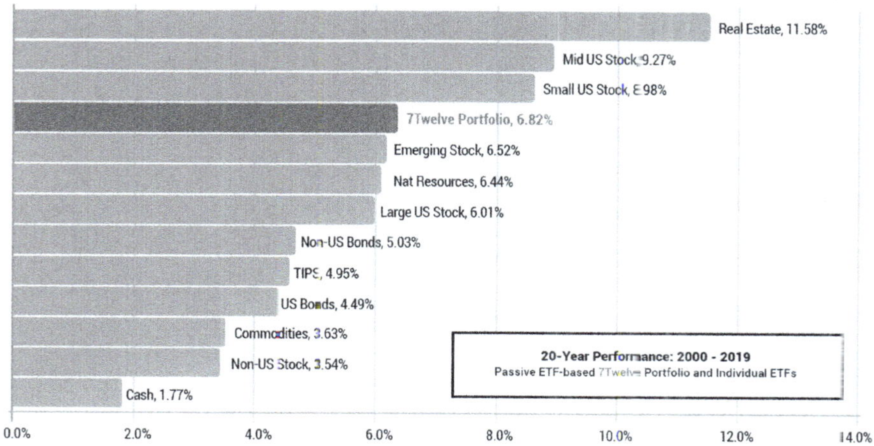

The name 7Twelve® is a registered trademark belonging to Craig L. Israelsen
Past performance of investment products or indexes does not guarantee future performance.

This is a very strategic and purposeful diversification. I see people mess up diversification every day. People understand the concept of diversification, but their actual implementation can end up being a costly mistake. This approach answers the question, "which part of the major market indexes should you be in?" with a simple, implementable, and well researched answer: "all of them equally." The historical risk and growth analysis we have just looked at validates that answer.

The approach my team and I take when implementing this strategy for clients is to keep the core 7Twelve concept, but make adjustments to capitalize on certain trends in the markets and economy. These adjustments can be very beneficial. They are "icing" on the 7Twelve "cake."

I hope you can see why I have been excited to share this strategy with you. Utilizing an equally-weighted 7Twelve strategy should give you a huge leap down the middle-of-the-road approach needed to effectively navigate growth and risk throughout retirement.

Chapter 28

Factor Investing

In this last chapter, we're going to specifically address using the second phase of strategic allocations, and how this can help you retire in a low-interest and potentially high-inflation-rate environment. Since you were previously inducted into the Hall family movie night, it's time for me to come clean. I didn't spoil the *whole* book when I told you that Chapter 27 was the most important. I *do* think it is the most important chapter, but it's not my favorite. What we are going to cover next is hands down my favorite part. It's not the most important, because it may only be a portion of your retirement account allocation. The 7Twelve will be the core of your allocation. Nonetheless, Phase 2 of Strategic Allocations could be a potentially powerful part of your retirement strategy when combined with the 7Twelve allocation.

What I call Phase 1 (7Twelve Multi-Asset) and Phase 2 (Factor Investing) are two distinct styles of strategic investing. They both try to answer the question, "What part of the markets should I be invested in?" What makes 7Twelve and Factor Investing work so well when implemented side by side in your retirement account, is that they answer that question from totally opposing viewpoints.

Recall with index fund allocations like the 7Twelve portfolio that there is an underlying belief that, "Markets are so efficient that there are no outliers to take advantage of—the only way to invest is by owning a broad-based index fund." This belief is applied to all the major traded investment markets by index investors. Most of all, it is applied religiously (frankly, fanatically) to the S&P 500, because the S&P 500 is the most widely traded, scrutinized, and analyzed index in the world. If there is one index where owning the whole index fund should perform better than only owning some assets of the index, it should be the S&P 500.

Keep your hands inside the vehicle, and hold on to your pocket protector. If you have given in to your inner index-investor-nerd at all, then this is gonna be crazy: On the next chart is substantial proof that there are splendid outlier segments (growth opportunities) in the most highly scrutinized index in the world.

Before we get too hasty, let me pause to reiterate—I understand the efficient market, "buy the index fund" approach. I'm not knocking it. Remember the last chapter. I celebrated with you the tremendous potential retirement benefits of buying all 12 major market index funds, and holding them for extended periods of time. For sure, take advantage of that strategy.

However, to assume that it is the only approach you want could be one of those mistakes that happen when you just don't know what you don't know. Those are the kind of mistakes I'm trying to help you avoid.

To introduce Phase 2 of strategic investing (Factor Investing), I want to tap into some of the amazing, innovative work done by John Lunt, the founder of Lunt Capital. Let's start with a "quilt chart" that John published in 2016. If my grandma could teach a rowdy 10-year-old Telton how to quilt (which she did) then I think I can teach you how to read a Factor Groups "quilt chart."

Here are the basics. The stocks that make up the S&P 500 each have identifying characteristics. These characteristics are called **Factors**. Common Factors of stocks are: Momentum, Quality, Value, Dividend, High Beta, and Low Volatility (Low Vol). Some groups of stocks are considered Momentum Stocks, some groups are considered Quality stocks, and some are considered Value stocks etc. Each group of stocks with similar characteristics are called a Factor Group. Different Factor Groups will act differently during any given economic environment. Each Factor

Group will have its own investment performance for the year. **Factor Investing** is, instead of investing in the whole index, only investing in the group of stocks (**Factor Group**) that all demonstrate a certain characteristic.

The upcoming quilt chart shows investment returns for the Factor Groups that make-up the S&P 500, year-by-year over 10 years.

To get your bearings, start with the 2005 column on the far left. The fourth box down indicates that the S&P 500 index, as a whole, grew 4.91% that year. The S&P 500 is an aggregate return of the stocks of all 500 companies.

Stock that has a characteristic of not fluctuating up and down very much is demonstrating a Low Volatility Factor (Low Vol). In the 2005 column, in the very bottom box, is the blended return of the group of stocks that demonstrated the Low Volatility (Low Vol) Factor. That year the Low Vol Factor Group of stocks grew 2.2%. In 2005, Low Vol had the lowest growth rate of all the Factor Groups. That's why it is in the bottom box.

In comparison, two above the Low Vol box in the 2005 column is the group of stocks from the S&P 500 that paid the best Dividends that year. That Dividend Factor Group grew by 3.69%. The group of stocks that demonstrated the Momentum Factor (the top box in the 2005 column) had the best gains, with 16.69%.

If you owned an S&P 500 index fund in 2005 your return would have been an average of all the stocks that make up the S&P 500. Your return would have been pretty close to the 4.91%, shown in the fourth box down. If you had owned a Factor Fund that only invested in the Momentum Factor stocks of the S&P 500 (the top box in 2005), your return would have been close to 16.69% that year. That is a huge difference. This potential opportunity for increased growth can help offset inflation in your retirement.

Take a moment to look at each column of this chart. First find the S&P 500 in each year. Mathematically, the S&P 500 will never be in the top box (best returns) or the bottom box (worst returns) because it is an average of all the Factor Groups. Then notice which Factor Groups of the S&P 500 outperformed and which underperformed in that year. You will see a substantial difference between the returns of the different Factors compared to the S&P 500 for the year.

2005	2006	2007	2008	2009	2010	2011	2012	2013	2014	2015	2016 thru 11/30	15 Yr Perf. Annualized
Momentum 16.69	Value 20.80	Quality 11.56	Low Vol. (21.41)	High Beta 57.35	High Beta 27.40	Low Vol. 14.78	High Beta 18.20	High Beta 41.24	Low Vol. 17.49	Momentum 5.56	High Beta 25.37	Dividend 9.78
Quality 7.54	Low Vol. 19.69	Momentum 9.89	Dividend (21.88)	Quality 26.72	Dividend 19.35	Quality 8.46	Value 17.68	S&P 500 32.39	Dividend 15.76	Low Vol. 4.34	Value 14.49	Low Vol. 9.20
Value 5.82	Dividend 17.30	S&P 500 5.49	Quality (31.14)	Dividend 26.56	Momentum 16.72	Dividend 8.33	Momentum 17.33	Momentum 31.42	S&P 500 13.69	Quality 2.11	Dividend 10.69	Quality 8.05
S&P 500 4.91	S&P 500 15.79	Value 1.99	Momentum (34.56)	S&P 500 26.46	Value 15.10	S&P 500 2.11	Dividend 16.94	Value 31.99	Quality 13.33	S&P 500 1.38	S&P 500 9.79	Momentum 7.18
Dividend 3.69	Quality 14.30	Low Vol. 0.58	S&P 500 (37.00)	Value 21.18	S&P 500 15.06	Momentum 1.60	Quality 16.09	Quality 31.66	High Beta 13.05	Dividend 0.93	Quality 9.21	S&P 500 6.62
High Beta 3.37	High Beta 9.97	High Beta (0.48)	Value (39.22)	Low Vol. 19.22	Quality 14.55	Value (0.48)	S&P 500 16.00	Dividend 32.27	Value 12.36	Value (3.13)	Low Vol. 7.61	Value 6.60
Low Vol. 2.20	Momentum 9.61	Dividend (2.07)	High Beta (60.32)	Momentum 17.24	Low Vol. 13.36	High Beta (18.01)	Low Vol. 10.30	Low Vol. 23.59	Momentum 11.23	High Beta (12.56)	Momentum 2.39	High Beta 3.83

Data from Morningstar. Indices used include S&P 500 Momentum TR USD, S&P 500 Low Volatility TR USD, S&P 500 TR USD, S&P 500 High Beta TR USD, S&P 500 Dividend Aristocrats TR USD, S&P 50 Value TR USD, and Russell 1000 Quality Factor TR USD. You cannot invest directly in an index.

The numbers in this chart (as with most "investment return" charts in this book) are purposefully taken from a few years ago. This allows us to focus on the theory, and also reminds us that this is a very successful *long-term* strategic approach to retirement investing. It is not dependent on this month, or this year, or this week's investment returns.

Now, let's look at the far-right column (15 Year Perf.) that is slightly separated from the rest of the chart. This is the 15-year average annual performance of each Factor Group. In the far-right column, the S&P 500 box is three from the bottom. You will see that the 15-year average return of the S&P 500, when this chart was created, was 6.62% per year.

The Low Vol Factor Group (the second-from-the top box in the 15 Year Perf. column) had an average annual return of 9.2%. When you compare that to the overall S&P 500 with a 6.6% return, that difference per year over 15 years is substantial and significant! Round numbers say that a 2.6% average outperformance per year, over 15 years, is an extra 39% in your account value. In addition to increased investment performance, this Low Vol Factor Group is composed of the stocks that have demonstrated the characteristic of having the least volatility. Lower volatility means lower risk. As previously discussed, strategies that have opportunities for growth, while reducing risk, are crucial.

A Low Vol Factor Fund is over long periods of time, the "poster child" of the potential increased returns available in Factor Group investing. Positioning a Low Vol Factor Fund next to a broadly diversified multi-asset portfolio (such as the 7Twelve), gives you the possibility to further increase your returns while lowering your volatility (risk).

Your retirement is going to be battling:

- A long life expectancy in retirement (which is wonderful and what we want, but it really reduces any wiggle room for making costly mistakes).
- Possibly being behind on your savings goals (statistically, most Baby Boomers are). Even upper middle-class folks are nervous about maintaining their lifestyle and outliving their money.
- The Low-Interest-Rate Environment
- Higher Inflation
- Volatility in the investment markets

Understanding the potential ability of these time-tested and research-based approaches, like combining 7Twelve and Factor

Fund investing, to help combat these headwinds can be very reassuring.

Let me teach you two more strategies utilizing Factors.

One potential strategy would be to use a Value Factor Fund during times of increasing inflation. As you now know, we are very likely in the midst of a period of increasing inflation. In Chapter 23 we briefly looked at the research by Fama and French, which suggests Value stocks have a tendency to perform better during higher inflationary periods. A Value Factor Fund, as part of your overall allocation, could be a way to capitalize on that trend in your retirement account.

For the second strategy, let's go back to the quilt chart. Start on the 15-Year Performance (15 Yr Perf.) column on the far-right side. If you had to choose just one or two Factor Funds to invest in for 15 years, it would probably be the top two boxes, Dividend payers and, of course the "poster child," Low Vol. Conversely, High Beta is the bottom box in the 15-Year Perf column. It is the "worst performing Factor Group" if you had held it alone for all 15 years. Yet, it has times with great returns.

Let's look through the rest of the "quilt chart."

Look at the factor that does far and away the best (top box) in 2009, 2010, 2013 and 2016. It is High Beta! We're not talking about beating the other factors by a little bit. High Beta was up 57% in the market rebound of 2009, compared to the closest competitor, Quality (the second box down), which grew 26%. That's impressive, especially from an S&P 500 index that is supposed to be "so efficient it has no outliers." High Beta returns in those years are definitely outliers. Then High Beta does it again in 2010, up 27.4% compared to the aggregate S&P 500 that is up 15.06%. That's nearly double. High Beta is in the top box in 2012 and then it way outperforms again in 2013 and 2016.

Using Factor Funds, allows you to be in the Factor Group of your choice at any time. You can easily and inexpensively switch to different factors year to year. There are seasons when market volatility is low, after a time of high risk, when consumer confidence is turning positive and growing, and economic growth is following. As we saw on the quilt chart, there is compelling historical evidence that investing in a High Beta Factor has the potential to substantially out-perform during these seasons. This could be another nice compliment to your long-term multi-asset strategy.

The Strategies I've shared with you do not rely on new companies, or speculative investments.

Bringing us full-circle to the first chapter of this book, I suggested that your retirement success would be founded, not on speculative investments but on utilizing strategies that have been well-researched and time-tested. Factor Investing (and of course the 7Twelve) fall into that category. The Strategies I've shared with you do not rely on new companies, or speculative investments. In fact, part of the reason the Factor Investing Strategy is so compelling is that it provides considerable opportunities for investment growth, while using the stocks of the largest, most highly scrutinized and regulated companies in the world.

My team and I have seen Factor Strategies be highly instrumental in our clients' success. I have been excited to share this concept with you. As you implement your own strategy to take advantage of the Value, Dividend, and Low Vol Factors, you can develop criteria that you are comfortable with for when it is the right season to move into and out of High Beta. John Lunt, whose innovative work I have utilized for this chapter, often teaches, "Live in the Low Vol neighborhood, and occasionally rent (or vacation) in High Beta." Utilizing a simple, implementable Factor Strategy like this, can help you take advantage of the opportunities that are available right in front of us.

Conclusion

Take Heart and Take Aways

We've come to the end of the book and your successfully retired self is thanking you. It's been a lot of fun to cover information about Fed Rates, mortgages, National Debt, Quantitative Easing, inflation, interest rates, Guaranteed Lifetime Withdrawal Benefits, major market indexes, the right type of broadly diversified multi-asset portfolios, and finally, Factor Investing. My team and I care about you and your retirement. I have truly tried to give you the knowledge and strategies you will need to have a high-quality retirement. On that note, let me tell you a funny story. It kind of pokes fun at me, but it's also very illustrative.

In my first year of college basketball at a junior college in Wyoming, the three "big guys" that were all competing for playing time were Robert, Dede, and me. I'm tall and athletic but Robert and Dede, they were something else. Robert was from Poland with a shaved head, very big, all muscle, and ended up playing for Bobby Knight during the Texas Tech years when they went to the Big Dance, and then he eventually played professional ball. Dede was from Africa, and was introduced to basketball in Belgium where his father was an ambassador. Leaping tall buildings wasn't superman, that was my teammate, Dede, a super talented guy.

Then you had Coach Davis, an animated character. He was a semi-pro football player turned college basketball coach. He was not a small dude either, but unlike Robert, he had quite a lot of untamed hair.

I'll do the best I can to imitate a scenario that played out a few times a week for the first months of practice. Coach Davis would turn to Robert and say "Robert, you're a machine. A machine!" He'd shake all over. His hair would bounce and shudder. "You're just so big and so strong, and when you run, you're just like a rocket!" he'd exclaim. Then he'd turn to Dede in a nearly-mesmerized trance, "You're like a gazelle, Dede, you jump so high and you're so quick, I've never seen a big man move like you" Coach Davis would say, as his hair swayed like grass in the savanna. Then finally he would turn to me and say, "and Tilton" (My name is TELton, but he would always say it TILton, which didn't bother me but it drove my teammates nuts and they always tried to correct him, to no avail.) He'd go on with all the compassion and conviction of a preacher saving a lost soul, "Tilton, I mean son, I mean really, son! Let me tell you. Son, you got a lot of... heart."

My teammates thought that was *Fuuuuunny*. I'd hear all about it in the dorm rooms, in the locker room, and in the classroom. It was humorous, I'll admit. But, I mean, we were in Wyoming, why couldn't he have compared me to a bull elk, an antelope, a cool tractor, or something somewhat impressive. But nope, I always got, "Son you got a lot of heart." It still makes me laugh, when I think about it.

Here's the cool part of the story. When it came time to pick the starters—the 5 guys Coach Davis wanted on the floor to give him the best chance to keep his livelihood—Coach always included me. It turns out some things require "a lot of heart."

As you can tell, I've never forgotten that experience and the lesson I learned about just caring, caring about what's right, the value of having a big heart to care about those around you. In the end, we all succeed together.

Let me leave you with three key takeaways.

Take Away Number One:

I think low interest rates are here to stay for a while, maybe a long while. The FOMC has indicated that. The stratospheric level of United States National Debt will make it very difficult on the Federal budget if interest rates rise. Even if inflation heats up, and your dollars are worth less, the FOMC has indicated they are not inclined to increase rates. Even if QE slows, 10-year Treasury yields rise and mortgage rates increase, the rates on savings and CDs will not be increasing. I think we have to plan for an extended period of low-interest on those types of conservative savings accounts. Pulling retirement income withdrawals from those types of accounts, generally, will only deplete your account before your life expectancy.

Take Away Number Two:

I think that getting your diversification right is going to be the key to a high-quality retirement, and getting diversification wrong can potentially be a costly mistake. Getting it right is NOT going to include things like arbitrarily selecting a few funds so you feel diversified. Diversification is NOT having a few different financial advisors that apply their prescription in their own way while you are in the middle with all the risk of an adverse reaction to multiple medications. Also diversification will probably not happen in the limited investment selection inside your 401k or workplace plan.

The right kind of retirement income diversification is going to require all hands on deck. It's going to mean:

- Maximizing your retirement income by correlating the timing and tax mitigation strategies on your
    - Social Security (and spouse's social security) if applicable
    - Pension (and spouse's pension) if applicable
    - Mortgage pay-off
    - Charitable contributions
    - Required minimum distributions

    (I saved these strategies for the next book)

- Utilizing, your newly-learned Phase 1 and 2 Strategic Allocations, with your retirement investments (401k's, 403b's, IRA's and Brokerage Accounts) in order to have
    - Growth opportunities to help offset inflation
    - Risk mitigation to preserve your account for a long life-expectancy

- Incorporating appropriate Short-Term strategies to
    - Maintain and grow (a little) your Emergency and Reserve funds

- Reducing risk (and stress) by appropriately utilizing long term guaranteed accounts such as
    - Indexed Annuities to avoid negative years in the market and participate in a portion of the positive years
    - Guaranteed Lifetime Withdrawal Benefits to create income security for your (and your spouse's) life while

still providing potential for account value growth and a death benefit for heirs

I'm convinced that you should consider all the tools available to you. Blending them to align with your retirement goals will require care, thought, and some work. But it's worth it. To quote from my Coach Davis days, it takes "a lot of heart" to win, but it is always worthwhile.

Speaking of heart, the final take-away, Number Three:

As you implement the knowledge and strategies necessary to provide *The Secure Solution* for your retirement, don't forget your legacy.

As you implement the knowledge and strategies necessary to provide *The Secure Solution* for your retirement, don't forget your legacy. We have talked a lot about the challenges to your retirement income plan in a low-interest, potentially higher-inflation environment. But I am a believer that we should still include in your plan what really matters to you. That's the point of your money and your retirement. In addition to travel and time with your loved ones, also include community and service. Do the extra planning to ensure your surviving spouse's income is going to be adequate down the road. That's the most important legacy. I have literally had nightmares after a prospective client comes to me, stuck in a very difficult financial situation because they didn't plan for financially taking care of the surviving spouse (statistically the wife). Please make Survivor Income part of your legacy planning. Also include any goals you have for your children, grandchildren, your favorite cause, your most cherished charities, etc. Those are the things you love. When we are planning out the dollars and income strategies, let's include the lasting legacy that you want to have. That is my final suggestion for *Creating a High-Quality Retirement in a Low-Interest-Rate World.*

Review Inquiry

Hey, it's Telton here.

I hope you've enjoyed the book, finding it super useful, helpful, and informative. I have a favor to ask you.

Would you consider giving it a five-star rating wherever you bought the book? Online book stores are more likely to promote a book when they feel good about its content, and reader reviews are a great barometer for a book's quality.

So please go to the website of wherever you bought the book, search for my name and the book title, and leave a five-star rating and a review. If able, perhaps consider adding a picture of you holding the book. That increases the likelihood your review will be accepted!

Many thanks in advance,
Telton W Hall

Will You Share the Love?

Get this book for a friend, associate or family member!

If you have found this book valuable and know others who would find it useful, consider buying them a copy as a gift. Special bulk discounts are available if you would like your whole team or organization to benefit from reading this. Just contact marty@afplanning.com, visit www.afplanning.com, or call 435-263-0550.

Would You Like Telton to Speak to Your Organization?

Book Telton W Hall Now!

Telton accepts a limited number of speaking engagements each year. To learn how you can bring his message to your organization, just contact marty@afplanning.com, visit www.afplanning.com, or call 435-263-0550.

Quick Reference Glossary

There is a whole new language associated with the Knowledge and Strategies you have learned in this book. Here I have collected a few vocabulary words and acronyms as a quick reference.

Annuity

There are many out-dated definitions floating around. Currently, this term denotes a savings, investment, or retirement product that has some type of benefit or guarantee provided by an insurance company. Current types of annuity offerings are so unique and distinct from each other they need to be understood individually. Broad assumptions about the advantages and disadvantages of the hundreds of diverse products that are called "annuities" can lead to costly mistakes. With that in mind, see Fixed Annuity, Indexed Annuity, Life-Pay Annuity, GLWB, and Variable Annuity for more focused definitions.

Bond

A generic term for Notes, Bills, Bonds, Debentures or any other type of debt investment. Bonds typically have an interest rate paid to the owner or investor of the bond and promise a return of the principal at the end of the bond term.

Certificate of Deposit (also called a Timed Account)
A Savings product offered by banks and Credit Unions. Has a set interest rate, and a specific length of time until funds can be withdrawn without paying a penalty. The penalty is usually so-many-months-worth of interest earned. In a low-interest-rate environment, the interest earned (hence the penalty) is typically not very high.

CPI
The Consumer Price Index tracks the average cost of goods and services. In order to measure how much prices are going up or down, the U.S. Bureau of Labor Statistics calculates the change in price of things like housing, clothes, transportation, food, healthcare, and education. The FOMC watches the CPI as a key measure of inflation.

Credit Union Deposit Insurance
Deposits at Federal Credit unions are backed (up to $250,000) by the National Credit Union Share Insurance fund, which is backed by the full faith and credit of the United States government.
Most, but not all, state-chartered Credit Unions are required to be federally insured. Federal insurance limits the amount of interest that can be paid on accounts. Higher-paying Credit Unions may not have federal insurance.

Cryptocurrency
Based on the theory and desire that central authority (governments and central banks) should not control or manipulate the value of currency or the currency holder, this is a digital medium of exchange where the owners are not identifiable, yet the transactions are public, and the databases and electronic records (blockchain) of ownership and transaction are protected by (hopefully) really strong encryption codes. It is called *crypto* because

the network of ownership and transactions is dependent on the encryption codes being strong enough to not get hacked. As of the writing of this book, a variety of cryptos are creating a lot of buzz among media and speculative investors.

Discount Rate

The interest rate set by the Federal Reserve Bank when lending to other large commercial and depository banks in the nation. The Fed uses this, much like the rest of the tools we discussed in this book, to either increase or decrease the money supply in order to boost or damper economic growth.

Duration

In this book this refers to **Bond Duration**. It s a combined measurement of how long until a bond investor gets their money back and how much the value of the bond will change when interest rates go up and down. It is stated in years, with "long-duration" indicating higher interest rate sensitivity, and "short-duration" bonds having less interest rate sensitivity.

EMBI

The Emerging Markets Bond Index represents the aggregate value of bonds that are issued in countries that are still developing their economies and their investment markets (Brazil, South Africa, China, Mexico are a few examples). This index reflects debt issued by those developing countries *themselves* as well as debt issued by *corporations* that are from those countries. Higher risk and higher yield is typically associated with this index.

Emergency Fund

Money that is held in a secure and accessible account to cover any unexpected expenses. Its job is *not* to earn money *nor* keep pace with inflation. Its job is to not fluctuate in value so it is there in case you ever need it. Having enough Emergency Fund money allows your other investment strategies to have a mid- to long-term time frame.

Exchange-Traded, Open, Public Markets

The centralized and regulated financial markets where traders, brokers, you, and I can buy and sell stocks, bonds, Treasuries, commodities, options, and funds composed of stock, bonds, Treasuries, commodities etc. The New York Stock Exchange is likely the most widely recognized.

Exchange-Traded Real Estate

Typically a Real Estate Investment Trust (REIT) that can be bought and sold at any time on the open market. See REIT.

Factor Investing

Consists of buying or selling a group of stocks that have the same identifying characteristics. These groups of stocks that share similar characteristics are called **Factor Groups**. This book focuses on selecting certain Factor Groups out of the S&P 500 Stock Index. Factor groups exist in all the Major Global Market Indexes and Factor Investing can be applied to those indexes as well—with compelling success I might add.

FDIC Insured

The Federal Deposit Insurance Corporation is backed by the full faith and credit of the United States government. It protects against the loss of insured deposits (up to $250,000) held at an FDIC-Insured Bank.

Federal Reserve System

The Central Banking System of the United States. It is composed of 12 Federal Banks and 24 Federal Branches throughout the United States. The actions of these banks are directed by the seven-member Board of Governors and the 12-member (seven of which are the Board of Governors) Federal Open Market Committee. Its role is to promote the health of the U.S. economy and stability of the U.S. financial system. One of the ways it accomplishes this is by utilizing tools to increase or decrease the interest rates throughout the economy.

Fed Funds Rate, Fed Funds Target Rate, or Fed Rate

The rate banks use when borrowing funds overnight from each other, or from a Federal Reserve Bank, to stay compliant with banking Reserve Requirements. This rate is set by the FOMC.

Fixed Annuity

Pays a fixed percentage rate of interest over a fixed time period.

FOMC

The Federal Open Market Committee is the decision-making and policy-announcing public face of the Federal Reserve Banks. The FOMC sets the target for the Fed Funds rate, and can direct Federal Reserve Banks to engage in Quantitative Easing.

GLWB

Guaranteed Lifetime Withdrawal Benefit is a type of annuity guarantee, backed by the claims-paying ability of the insurance company, that for an additional cost provides single-lifetime or joint, spousal-lifetime retirement income. When used with a Variable Annuity the guaranteed lifetime retirement income can potentially increase, but it will not decrease. Any unused funds in the account at death pass to the beneficiaries.

Great Recession

The largest financial and economic meltdown since the Great Depression, this global economic, real estate, employment, and investment market decline started in 2007, plummeted in 2008, and technically ended in June of 2009, but it impacted careers, retirement savings, real estate prices, and emotional well-being across the globe for much longer. The pressure and stress of this time period just about crushed the author of this work (and some of the readers of it). Not to worry though; it also developed, refined, and tested the strategies presented in this book.

High Interest Saving Account

Should probably be called a Teensy-Bit-Higher-Interest-Than-a-Regular-Savings Account in this low-interest-rate environment. By limiting transactions this type of FDIC or Credit Union Insured account provides slightly higher interest rates. This might be a good type of account for your Emergency Fund.

Index

Index technically means “a list.” An investment index is a set of rules that, when applied to all the available investments, gives you a list, or a group, of investments. Tracking the price changes of this list of investments makes it very convenient to measure the purely mathematical positive or negative performance of these investments at any given time. This creates a hypothetical investment. It also provides the list of investments for an Index Fund to purchase in order to create a real (non-hypothetical) investment.

Indexed Annuity, Fixed-Indexed Annuity, Equity-Indexed Annuity

Provides the investor the benefit of having no negative years in exchange for only receiving a portion of the investment growth in positive years.

Index Fund

Attempts to mirror the investment list of a specific index in order to provide an investor the means of achieving similar investment results to the pure math of the Index.

Inflation

When prices of goods increase and/or the value and purchasing power of your money decreases.

Interest Rate Sensitivity

Indicates how much a bond's value will increase (when interest rates go down) or decrease (when interest rates move up). Duration is a major component of this.

Large Cap

Refers to companies whose stock capitalization (the number of stock shares multiplied by price per share) is over $10 billion.

LIBOR

London Inter-Bank Offering Rate is the average rate (technically called a trimmed-mean) of interest that large global banks charge each other for short-term loans.

Life-Pay Annuity

A type of annuity that is still used in many "older-style" pension systems. It provides a single-lifetime or joint, spousal-lifetime retirement income payment. The payments are guaranteed for life. Any unused funds in the account at death stay with the annuity or pension.

Major Market Indexes

Represent the largest investment opportunities that exist on exchange-traded markets around the globe: U.S. Large Cap

Stocks, U.S. Mid Cap Stocks, U.S. Small Cap Stocks, Developed Non-U.S. Stocks, Emerging Non-U.S. Stocks, Global Real Estate, Natural Resources, Commodities, U.S. Bonds, U.S. Inflation Protected Bonds, Non-U.S. Bonds, and Cash or Cash Equivalents.

Mid Cap
Refers to companies whose stock capitalization (the number of stock shares multiplied by price per share) is in the $2 to $10 billion range.

Monetary Policy
The Federal Reserve Banks' regulation of the amount of, and ease of access to, money in the economy. To accomplish their money supply goals, the Fed uses Open Market Operations, The Discount Rate, and Reserve Requirements.

Money Market Account
Interest bearing account at a bank or credit union. These accounts often have withdrawal limits of three times a month in trade off for a slightly higher interest rate. These will be FDIC or Credit Union insured. Please note there are also money market mutual funds that are the same basic concepts, but do not have the FDIC or Credit Union Insurance.

Mortgage Bonds
Most mortgage providers bundle their mortgages, once originated, and sell them in the public markets as a mortgage bond. A loan-service interfaces with the real estate owner who took out the mortgage to ensure proper escrow payments and property insurance are in place, but it is an investor who actually owns the mortgage. It is possible for you to have a mortgage on your

home and own your mortgage in the bond fund you hold in your investment account.

Multi-Asset Portfolio

This type of portfolio blends investments from different segments of the investment market and areas of the world, as well as investments with different strengths, weaknesses, stability and fluctuations. As demonstrated by the 7Twelve portfolio, this would include funds representing a mix of U.S. stock, U.S. bonds, non-U.S. stock, non-U.S. bonds, Real Estate Natural Resources, Commodities and Cash.

National Debt, Government Debt, Public Debt

The amount of money that the United States government has borrowed and promised to pay back with interest.

Open Market Operations

When the Federal Reserve Banks engage in buying and selling primarily U.S. Treasury securities, as well as other securities (typically bonds) in public investment markets in order to regulate the supply of money that is available.

Overlap

When two funds that are tracking different indexes end up having the same or very similar holdings.

Performance

A term used to indicate the level of total increase or decrease an investment experiences during a given time frame.

Prime Rate

The rate that large U.S. banks will give their most creditworthy customers.

Quantitative Easing

When the FOMC directs Federal Reserve Banks to purchase substantial amounts of U.S. Debt and other bonds in order to create and maintain low interest rates and low yields.

REIT

A Real Estate Investment Trust is a means for an investor to own an interest in multiple properties at once with no maintenance or management requirements. A REIT can be focused or it can be highly diversified across various property types around the globe. An Exchange-Traded-REIT is liquid and can be sold on the exchange traded market.

Reserve Account

This is my nickname for funds that are in addition to your Emergency Fund, yet have not been dedicated to creating your retirement income. A Reserve Account can be used to fund a larger expense that is still a few years down the road, or used as additional funds to help offset inflation later in retirement.

Reserve Requirements

An amount of funds, set by the Fed, that banks must keep available in order to meet demands for withdrawals.

Return

A term used to indicate the level of total increase or decrease an investment experiences during a given time frame.

Risk

For our non-technical purposes, this refers to negative performance of investments.

S&P 500 Stock Index

The Standard and Poor's 500 Index is a widely known barometer of the Large Cap stocks of the U.S. stock market. An Index Fund that tracks the S&P 500 Index holds the stock of the 500 largest publicly-traded companies in the U.S. Because a few of these companies have multiple share classes, there are technically 505 holdings—but it still represents 500 companies.

Savings Account

Interest-bearing account held at a bank or Credit Union

Small Cap

Refers to companies whose stock capitalization (the number of stock shares multiplied by price per share) is in the $250 million to $2 billion range.

Standard Deviation

Technical formula for measuring the level of movement of an investment. For our non-technical purposes, this refers to the risk of having negative performance in your investments.

Strategic Allocations

These types of allocations decide which investments to invest in and adjust those areas occasionally, but stay invested "in" the markets all the time.

Survivor Income Planning

Helps ensure the surviving spouse's income is going to be adequate when the other spouse dies. Statistically one spouse (usually the wife) is going to outlive the other by at least several years. At the first spouse's death, changes to social security payments, pension payments, and retirement account withdrawals can potentially, and sometimes drastically, lower the surviving spouse's retirement income.

Tactical Allocations

This allocation moves money from cash ("out" of the markets) to investments ("in" the markets) and back again following self-established guidelines.

TIPS

Treasury Inflation Protected Securities are National Debt issued by the U.S. Treasury designed to preserve the value of your dollar during times of inflation. TIPS pay a fixed interest rate, and their value increases with the CPI.

Treasuries

Treasuries are issued by the U.S. Treasury in the form of Treasury bonds, bills, and notes. These bonds, bills, and notes are considered highly secure investments because they are backed by the U.S. government's ability to tax the U.S. economy.

United States Treasury

Manages the funds of the U.S. government. This management includes collecting taxes, paying bills, and issuing what you and I call National Debt or Government Debt. The Treasury calls it "Public Debt." The U.S. Treasury is commissioned to collect taxes. When the tax revenue is insufficient to cover government spending, the U.S. Treasury issues National Debt called Treasuries.

Variable Annuity

A contract between you and the insurance company that allows you to make investment selections from the available investment sub-accounts. Your annuity contract's value will fluctuate up and down based on the sub-account's investment portfolio performance. Death Benefit Guarantees and Guaranteed Lifetime Withdrawal Benefits (see GLWB definition) are backed by the financial strength of the insurance company.

Volatility

For our non-technical purposes, this refers to the potential for investments to have negative performance.

Yield

The percentage return based on the purchase price (usually of a bond) in the open market.

Investment Disclosures

- Asset allocation and diversification do not ensure a profit or prevent a loss in a declining market. They are methods used to help manage investment risk. There is no assurance that a diversified portfolio will perform better than a non-diversified portfolio.
- References to investment returns and yields are for hypothetical, illustrative purposes only. Actual results will vary. Any market indexes shown are unmanaged and considered representative of their respective markets. Individuals cannot directly invest in an index. Past performance is not a guarantee of future results.
- Investing and investment strategies involve risk including the potential loss of principal. The stated information does not claim to be a complete description of the securities, markets or developments referred to in the book.
- Equity investments including index funds are subject to market fluctuations and may be worth more or less than when originally purchased. Certain index funds will have additional risks depending on the markets and/or stocks that the index fund represents. These risks might include exposure to increased volatility, leverage, illiquidity, currency exchanges, political and economic uncertainties, and commodity price fluctuations.

- Bonds are exposed to credit and interest rate risk (when rates rise, bond fund prices generally fall). Lower-rated bonds are subject to greater fluctuations in value and are more at risk of default of income and principal.
- Index Mutual Funds and ETFs (Exchange-Traded Funds) are sold by prospectus. Investors should carefully consider the investment objectives, risks, charges, and expenses of these funds before investing. This and other important information is contained in the prospectus, which can be obtained from the mutual fund company or your financial advisor and should be read carefully before investing.
- Variable Annuities (VAs) are long term investments designed for retirement purposes. VAs involve risk and are offered by prospectus only. Investors should carefully consider the investment objectives, risks, charges, and expenses of the VA and its underlying investment options. The prospectus contains this and other important information and should be carefully read before investing.
- Annuity withdrawals may be subject to income tax, and if taken prior to age 59½, a 10% federal tax penalty may apply. Early withdrawals may be subject to additional charges by the insurance company.
- Death benefits and other annuity riders may be subject to additional costs and restrictions. Guarantees, death benefits and riders are backed by the claims-paying ability of the issuing insurance company and are subject to their terms and conditions. Annuities are not FDIC insured.

About the Author

Telton Hall, CFP® is a husband, father, retirement planning expert, small town boy at heart, nationally published author, sought-after speaker, former college basketball player, founder, owner, and team member of Utah-based Advanced Financial Planning LLC, hiking enthusiast, Jesus follower, business leader, team builder, and, to the core, Telton is an educator. It is rumored among his dinner guests that he can play the piano and sing a few George Strait songs, but that is yet to be verified on the internet.

Telton grew up on a small ranch near Zion National Park, Utah. In addition to learning how to haul hay and fix fence, at age nine Telton's mom taught him about this thing she called a "mutual fund." He was captivated! This led him on an investing journey from Elementary school through high school. Telton attended Eastern Wyoming Junior College, and served a two-year, Spanish-speaking church mission. Upon returning, he played Division 1 basketball for and graduated summa cum laude from Southern Utah University. While at SUU Telton simultaneously prepared for a career in higher education and coaching or financial planning.

He received "The Outstanding Graduate in English Education" award from the English Department. At the same time, he passed federal and state licensing exams, and began working part time selling insurance and (can you guess it?) mutual funds. He was inspired to become a financial advisor when he learned about the complex retirement challenges facing the Baby Boomers—good folks just like his parents.

His passion and expertise is educating and helping upper middle class families accomplish their retirement dreams. As a Certified Financial Planner™ professional and through thousands of real-life, real-people retirement planning sessions, he has become the go-to expert and sought-after presenter for teaching courses on pension planning decisions, social security maximization, investment allocations for retirement, and retirement tax strategies.

He has remained involved with his local alma mater through sponsoring the SUU Everyday Leader Scholarship, mentoring, and as an Advisory Board Member for the SUU Investment Scholars.

Learn more about Telton and the Advanced Financial Planning, LLC Team at: www.afplanning.com

Made in the USA
Monee, IL
19 October 2026

66036205R00118